# A Practical Guide to Corporate Governance

David W. Duffy, FCA

Chartered
Accountants
Ireland

Published in 2014 by
Chartered Accountants Ireland
Chartered Accountants House
47–49 Pearse Street
Dublin 2
www.charteredaccountants.ie

ISBN 978-1-908199-84-3

Typeset by Datapage
Printed by Turner's Printing Company, Longford, Ireland

*This book is dedicated to my parents Walter Nathaniel Duffy and Ursula Joy Duffy to whom I owe everything.*

# Contents

# Preface

The increasing focus on corporate governance in Ireland is a direct result of the challenging times we have experienced as a country over the last five years or so. The lessons learnt will assist in advancing the practice of corporate governance, which is fundamental to our economy and future prosperity.

While supported by various codes of governance providing the guidance required at a more detailed level, good governance is based on values and ethics, which provide the resilience required to help organisations navigate more uncertain times. It is the 'tone from the top' that will determine the success or otherwise of any organisation.

This guide seeks to improve corporate governance in Ireland in a very practical manner. It provides a wealth of valuable and practical information that can be applied to any organisation, regardless of nature, size or complexity.

This resource will be especially useful for chairs, non-executive directors, Company Secretaries, executive directors, members of executive management teams and those who aspire to become directors. It will enable directors to play a more active and informed role in the companies with which they are associated.

The development of this publication would not have been possible without the contribution of the many individuals I interviewed who gave freely of their time, experience and insights. To them I owe a huge debt of gratitude. (You know who you are.) I would like to thank them for their common-sense suggestions which give this guide a sharper and more practical edge.

This book is based on the insight, knowledge and know-how of my colleagues at Prospectus in providing practical corporate governance advice to organisations. To them past and present, a big thanks.

I would also like to thank to Peter Duffy (no relation!) whose commitment and research, contributed enormously to the insight and quality of this publication.

I hope this book will advance the practice of corporate governance in Ireland and make a real difference.

David W. Duffy, FCA
October 2014

# 1.

# Introduction

- Context
- The Rationale for this Guide
- What is Corporate Governance?
- History and Evolution of Corporate Governance
- Recent Developments in Ireland
- How to Use this Guide

## Context

The events of September 2008 and the subsequent crash shook the global financial and corporate system to its core. As the OECD has stated:

> "The financial crisis can be to an important extent attributed to failures and weaknesses in corporate governance arrangements which did not serve their purpose to safeguard against excessive risk taking."[1]

Ireland witnessed the collapse of many of its seemingly most stable financial institutions, raising concerns over the robustness and integrity of the underlying governance processes and risk management. The crash, aside from disintegrating global capital markets, forced many organisations to reflect on their governing structures and internal controls.

The financial crisis unearthed in Ireland a series of scandals concerning board failures, conflicts of interest, greed, information breakdowns and much else besides. As a result, the succeeding years have witnessed numerous crises and subsequent regulatory changes in the field of corporate governance; the roles and responsibilities of boards and directors have come under increased and very public scrutiny as never before.

## The Rationale for this Guide

The first edition of this guide (published by the author in 2004) provided a step-by-step reference guide to improving the practice of corporate governance. This latest new and expanded edition goes further by focusing on areas that require a more specific focus given the experiences of the last five or six years.

There are new chapters on ethics and values, board reporting and reflections on improving corporate governance. Included in the appendices are additional reference resources on: matters reserved for the board, draft terms of reference for the executive management team and a draft charter on ethics and values. Finally, we have included some case studies from diverse sectors of the economy to

[1] OECD, 'The Corporate Governance Lessons from the Financial Crisis', 2009.

highlight the consequences of inadequate corporate governance, policies, structures and processes.

More generally, we have updated the roles and responsibilities of those elements within governance structures in line with new governance codes and legislation.

This guide is designed to provide chairmen, directors, company secretaries, members executive of management teams and potential board members with a practical resource, explaining the key building blocks to improving corporate governance and allowing them to play a more active and informed role in their companies.

> *Note*: the term 'company' also means organisation in this book. The general principles and practices of corporate governance discussed in this book also apply to other organisations, such as non-profits, charities and organisations established under statute not withstanding their differing legal bases.

## What is Corporate Governance?

The *Cadbury Report* defines corporate governance as "the system by which organisations are directed and controlled".[2] More specifically, it is concerned with the "management of management": the structures and processes in place at the top of an organisation for decision-making, accountability, controls and behaviour.

Corporate governance is a complex topic and much has been written of it in recent years. Regardless of the type, size or purpose of a company, all directors have a responsibility to ensure that their corporate governance is fit for purpose.

## History and Evolution of Corporate Governance

Since the original *Cadbury Report* in 1992, corporate governance has expanded its scope and has had a profound influence in evolving regulation requirements and in the emphasis placed on their effective use.

---

[2] *Report of the Committee on the Financial Aspects of Corporate Governance* ('The Cadbury Report' (Gee Publishing, 1992)), para. 2.7.

Numerous reports in the 1990s led to the publication in June 1998 of the *Combined Code on Corporate Governance* (the *'Combined Code'*), which was in turn revised in 2003 and 2008.

However, following the financial crash, the *Walker Review*[3] prompted a new *UK Corporate Governance Code*, issued by the Financial Reporting Council (FRC) in 2010, amended in 2012 and updated in 2014. The *Walker Review* also led to the publication of the *UK Stewardship Code*,[4] applicable to firms who manage assets on behalf of institutional investors.

Beyond this, the Irish Stock Exchange published its own "Irish Corporate Governance Annex" in 2010, to supplement the *UK Corporate Governance Code*, focusing particularly on Irish PLCs.[5] The Irish Central Bank has also issued its own codes, including one for credit institutions and insurance undertakings, designed to combat failures in the Irish banking system.[6] Uniquely, this code is enforceable by legislation, indicative of the Irish Government's reformist approach to corporate governance.

Furthermore, in 2011 the EU issued a green paper, *The EU Corporate Governance Framework*,[7] designed to enhance transparency and operations across the EU.

The key recommendations of each of these reports and codes are outlined in **Appendix A1** of this guide.

### Chronology of Reports and Publications on Corporate Governance: 1992–2011

| Publication | Date | Focus |
|---|---|---|
| *The Cadbury Report* | December 1992 | • Financial aspects of corporate governance;<br>• control and reporting functions of the board and the role of auditors. |

[3] *A review of corporate governance in UK banks and other financial industry entities: Final recommendations* (26 November 2009).
[4] Financial Reporting Council 2010.
[5] Irish Stock Exchange, *Main Securities Market Listing Rules and Admission to Trading Rules*, Appendix 4, "Irish Corporate Governance Annex" (ISE, 2011).
[6] Central Bank of Ireland, *Corporate Governance Code for Credit Institutions and Insurance Undertakings* (Central Bank of Ireland, 2010).
[7] COM(2011) 164 final Brussels, 5.4.2011.

| | | |
|---|---|---|
| *The Greenbury Report*[8] | July 1995 | • Directors' remuneration;<br>• fundamental principles of accountability, transparency, and linkage of rewards to performance. |
| *The Hampel Committee Report*[9] | January 1998 | • Review of the findings of *Cadbury* and *Greenbury*;<br>• the role of directors;<br>• directors' remuneration;<br>• shareholders and the AGM;<br>• accountability and audit. |
| *The Combined Code on Corporate Governance* | June 1998 | • Amalgamated the *Cadbury* and *Greenbury* reports along with its own recommendations. |
| *The Turnbull Report*[10] | September 1999; revised 2005 | • Guidance for directors on the *Combined Code*;<br>• internal control;<br>• risk management. |
| *The Higgs Report*[11] | January 2003 | • Role of the non-executive director. |
| *The Smith Report*[12] | January 2003 | • Role of the Audit Committee. |
| *The Combined Code on Corporate Governance*[13] | Revised July 2003 | • Updated to reflect recent developments, especially the *Smith* and *Higgs Reports*. |

[8] *Directors' Remuneration: Report of a Study Group Chaired by Sir Richard Greenbury* (Gee Publishing, 1995).
[9] *The Committee on Corporate Governance – Final Report* (Gee Publishing, 1998).
[10] *Internal Control: Guidance for Directors on the Combined Code* (ICAEW 1999: FRC revised 2005).
[11] *Review of the Role and Effectiveness of Non-executive Directors* (Department of Trade and Industry, 2003).
[12] *Audit Committees: Combined Code Guidance* (FRC, 2003).
[13] *The Combined Code on Corporate Governance* (FRC, 2003).

| | | |
|---|---|---|
| *The Combined Code on Corporate Governance*[14] | Revised June 2008 | • Provisions on the design of performance related remuneration;<br>• guidance on liability of non-executive directors;<br>• disclosure or corporate governance arrangements. |
| *The Walker Review* | November 2009 | • Review into the effectiveness of Board practices and risk management at Board level. |
| *The UK Corporate Governance Code*[15] | June 2010 (revised September 2012) | • Sets out standards of good practice in relation to Board leadership and effectiveness, remuneration, accountability and relations with shareholders. |
| *The UK Stewardship Code*[16] | July 2010 (revised September 2012) | • Sets out good practice on the engagement between institutional investors and companies. |
| *Corporate Governance Code for Credit Institutions and Insurance Undertakings*[17] | November 2010 | • Minimum statutory requirements for governance of banks and insurance companies in Ireland. |
| "Irish Corporate Governance Annex"[18] | December 2010 | • Irish Stock Exchange supplementary code to the UK code, concerning Irish listed companies. |
| *The EU Corporate Governance Framework*[19] | April 2011 | • Green Paper setting out corporate governance plans for Europe. |

[14] *The Combined Code on Corporate Governance* (FRC, 2008).
[15] *The UK Corporate Governance Code* (FRC, 2012).
[16] *The UK Stewardship Code* (FRC, 2012).
[17] *Governance Code for Credit Institutions and Insurance Undertakings* (Central Bank of Ireland, 2010).
[18] Irish Stock Exchange, *Main Securities Market Listing Rules and Admission to Trading Rules*, Appendix 4, "Irish Corporate Governance Annex" (ISE, 2011).
[19] EU Green Paper COM(2011) 164 final Brussels, 5.4.2011.

| The UK Corporate Governance Code[20] | September 2014 | • Improves quality of information investors receive about the long-term health of the company;<br>• requirement to include a 'viability statement';<br>• remuneration of key executives to be designed to promote the long-term success of the company. |
|---|---|---|

## Recent Developments in Ireland

### *Charities Act 2009*

The Charities Act 2009 was enacted to reform the law relating to charities and provides for the creation of a Charities Regulatory Authority and – for the first time in Ireland – a Register of Charities. The Act aims to ensure greater accountability, protect against fraudulent abuse of charitable status and to enhance public trust, confidence and transparency in charities and their trustees. The Act has significant implications for all charities and their trustees, introducing a number of charity law offences. It provides a definition of 'charitable purposes' and makes it an offence for any organisation that is not registered as a charity to present itself as one. The Act also creates a statutory requirement to **ensure** compliance with all the legal obligations, focusses on better administration and the requirement to file an annual activity report. The Register of Charities, on which all charities must be registered, was established in 2014.

Furthermore, Irish company law requires that charities that are registered as companies submit annual accounts to the Companies Registration Office (CRO). Under the new regulatory framework, the CRO will submit these annual accounts to the Charity Regulatory Authority.

---

[20] *The UK Corporate Governance Code* (FRC, 2014). (**Note:** "*The UK Corporate Governance Code 2014* applies to accounting periods beginning on or after 1 October 2014 and applies to all companies with a Premium listing of equity shares regardless of whether they are incorporated in the UK or elsewhere.")

A different set of requirements will apply to charities that are not registered as companies:

- Unincorporated charities will be required to submit an annual statement of accounts to the Regulator.
- Where the gross income or expenditure of an unincorporated charitable organisation in a financial year does not exceed €100,000, the charity may prepare an income and expenditure account and a statement of its assets and liabilities.
- Charities that are not companies which receive less than €10,000 in a financial year will be exempt from filing annual accounts.

These bodies are still required to submit an annual activity report. The details of this have not been finalised.

## EU Green Paper 2011

In 2011, the European Commission initiated an evaluation of the effectiveness of the current corporate governance rules for companies in the EU. It also carried out an online public consultation on the future of EU company law, which generated a large number of responses from a wide variety of stakeholders. This led to the publication of an EU green paper in 2011, *The EU Corporate Governance Framework,* which provides the background to an 'Action Plan' issued in December 2012: *European company law and corporate governance – a modern legal framework for more engaged shareholders and sustainable companies.*[21]

The green paper seeks to improve transparency of directors' remuneration, giving shareholders the right to vote on these policies. There is also a proposal to improve the transparency of conflict of interest frameworks and encourage transnational employee share ownership. Further proposals include assessing the need for cross-border transfer of companies' registered offices and assessing the need for cross-border mergers.

The green paper highlights the need to clarify the role of the chairman and gives guidance on board composition, evaluation,

[21] Communication from the Commission to the European Parliament, the Council, The European Economic and Social Committee and the Committee of the Regions, *Action Plan: European company law and corporate governance – a modern legal framework for more engaged shareholders and sustainable companies* (Strasbourg, 12.12.2012, COM(2012) 740 final).

remuneration and risk management. It also examines the role of shareholders and the use of the 'comply or explain' approach.

Lastly, the green paper questions whether the EU should have a differentiated approach for different sizes and types of unlisted companies.

In 2012, the European Commission adopted an 'Action Plan' outlining future initiatives in the areas of company law and corporate governance. The aim of the Action Plan is to encourage and facilitate long-term shareholder engagement, by increasing the level of transparency between companies and their shareholders and by simplifying cross-border operations of undertakings in the EU. It seeks to improve corporate governance in EU listed and unlisted companies.

In April 2014, the European Commission announced a package of measures to improve corporate governance for listed companies within the EU. The proposals aim to encourage long-term shareholder engagement and to improve corporate governance reporting by listed companies.

The package includes:

• a proposal to revise the Shareholder Rights Directive;
• a recommendation on the quality of corporate governance reporting – the 'comply or explain' principle.

The *UK Corporate Governance Code* has been instrumental in spreading best boardroom practice throughout the listed sector since it was first issued in 1992. It operates on the principle of 'comply or explain'. Listed companies are required under the Financial Conduct Authority Listing Rules either to comply with the provisions of the Code or to explain to investors in their next annual report why they have not done so. If shareholders are not content, they should engage with the company. If this is unsatisfactory, they can use their rights, including the power to appoint and remove directors, to hold the company to account.

The Commission is of the view that there are "shortcomings in the way the 'comply or explain' principle is applied" by EU listed companies. Specifically, it highlights that "companies often do not provide appropriate explanations when they depart from corporate governance codes".

The recommendation on the quality of corporate governance reporting aims to "provide guidance on how listed companies should explain their departures from the recommendations of the relevant corporate governance codes". The recommendation will not be legally binding, but is intended to "improve the overall quality of corporate governance statements published by companies".

## The Companies Bill 2012

The Companies Bill 2012 seeks to consolidate and simplify 16 previous Companies Acts, dating from 1963 to 2012, into one statute, completely reorganising and reforming Irish company law. The Bill was published in December 2012 and is now in consultation stage and is expected to become law in 2015.

The new Act will place the private company limited by shares ('LTD'), which comprise roughly 90% of Irish companies, at the centre of the legislation. Parts 1 to 15 of the Bill are concerned with the LTD, while Parts 16 to 25 deal with other types of company, such as the PLC, the designated activity company ('DAC'), the company limited by guarantee ('CLG') and the unlimited company.

The first Part of the Bill provides an exhaustive statement of the law applicable to private companies. The Bill simplifies the process for establishing a LTD and allows the LTD to have "full and unlimited capacity", abolishing the doctrine of *ultra vires* and the need for an objects clause. Key features include:

- LTDs may have only one single director and directors' duties will be codified and simplified. The company must also have a Company Secretary.
- LTDs will now be able to engage in mergers and divisions.
- Many of the provisions typically set out in a company's Articles of Association will become incorporated into the Bill/Act requiring companies to only set out exceptions to the norm in their constitution.

Directors of all PLCs and certain CLGs, DACs and LTDs with a balance sheet exceeding €12.5 million and turnover of over €25 million will be required to complete a compliance statement. This is a more proportionate approach than in the Companies (Auditing and Accounting)

Act 2003, under which directors had to complete a compliance statement if the balance sheet totalled more than €7.6 million and turnover of €15.2 million.

Under the new Act, the enforcement of directors' duties will be revised and updated, and the restrictions on directors' loans will be retained along the lines of those in the Companies Act 1990.

The Companies Bill codifies directors' eight main fiduciary duties for the first time (which are highlighted in **Chapter 4**, Building Blocks of Corporate Governance) and also makes changes to accounting and financial statements provisions (these new accounting and reporting requirements are covered in **Chapter 5**, Board Reporting).

## How to Use this Guide

This guide is intended to be a resource for anybody who needs to know more about the practicalities of corporate governance.

**Chapter 1** provides an overview of the background and history of corporate governance beginning with the seminal work in 1992 by Sir Adrian Cadbury called *The Cadbury Report,* which for the first time brought a focus on the financial aspects of corporate governance, control and reporting functions of the board, to the present day, the EU Green Paper on the corporate governance framework and the *UK Corporate Governance Code.*

**Chapter 2** outlines the key challenges for **boards of directors**, namely:

- board composition
- risk management
- board information
- board commitment
- board productivity.

**Chapter 3** focuses on ethics and values and provides insight into how important the role of the chairman is in setting the ethical and moral compass for the organisation. Given the apparent ethical and moral deficit for many organisations over the last 10 years, this chapter has particular relevance and should be the starting point for establishing the appropriate corporate governance in an organisation.

**Chapter 4** sets out the building blocks that make up the corporate governance framework. These are as follows:

- chief executive
- executive management team
- board
- chairman
- non-executive directors
- executive directors
- Company Secretary
- board committees.

The chapter contains essential information on the structures associated with each of these roles and functions and a section on each, including the following information:

- role of the person or group of people;
- responsibilities of this person or group;
- key legal considerations;
- insights and practical suggestions into the challenges and issues related to the role;
- key questions to be considered by the chairman, directors, etc.

The roles and responsibilities outlined for each element of the framework may need to be modified to take into account the specific circumstances of each company or organisation.

A corporate governance calendar is also provided as a reference for key events and their timing – for example the annual general meeting, board meetings and executive management team meetings – during a typical year of a company.

**Chapter 5** covers board reporting, focussing on what management information a director needs to be provided with to carry out his or her role. Just about every code of governance refers to what the Financial Reporting Council (FRC) describes as the need for the board to be "supplied in a timely manner with information in a form and of a quality appropriate to enable it to discharge its duties".[22]

**Chapter 6** addresses the topic of risk management. A critical part of any director's role is knowing what are the key risks the organisation

---

[22] *UK Corporate Governance Code* (FRC, 2014), para. B5.

is exposed to and how they should be mitigated, managed and monitored.

**Chapter 7** deals with how to evaluate board performance. Boards should undertake formal and rigorous evaluations of their overall performance and that of individual directors. These evaluations are of enormous benefit as they can improve the performance and accountability of boards. Given the effort and cost that goes into preparing for and holding each board meeting, it is important to look back on a regular basis to assess how well the board has performed and to what extent it has added real value to the company.

Finally, **Chapter 8** looks at the future of corporate governance and specific areas that merit attention to improve performance.

# 2.

# Corporate Governance Challenges

- Introduction
- Board Composition
- Risk Management
- Board Information
- Board Commitment
- Board Productivity

# Introduction

Increased uncertainty, financial instability, tougher regulatory requirements and greater public scrutiny mean that there are more challenges than ever facing boards of directors.

All forms of legal entities, from PLCs to private companies and from statutory bodies to non-profits, have witnessed failures in strategy development, implementation, decision-making processes, governance and risk management.

This chapter outlines the main reasons for these, through what we consider to be the **five critical challenges in corporate governance** today:

- board composition
- risk management
- board information
- board commitment
- board productivity.

# Board Composition

## *The Right People*

One of the most common weaknesses of Irish boards is the perceived lack of skilled and experienced individuals sitting at the boardroom table. The challenge for all organisations is to ensure that the skills and experience of those on the board are aligned with the needs of the organisation and its strategic direction.

According to an Institute of Directors in Ireland report in 2012, 21% of directors under 50 years of age do not feel they are adequately qualified to be on their boards.[1] Indeed, many of the directors we interviewed for this book stressed that board members often lacked the financial and sectoral knowledge as well as the soft skills necessary for being an effective director, leading to poorly informed decision-making in particular.

---

[1] *50 Under 50: A Research Report with 50 Directors Under 50 Years of Age* (Institute of Directors in Ireland, September 2012).

At the same time, there is no doubt that there is available to Irish companies a large pool of talented and experienced directors both in Ireland and overseas. The challenge for boards today is to tap into this pool effectively by ensuring those appointed have the appropriate experience and know-how to make a real contribution.

## Perceived 'Clubiness'

Boards need to avoid the perception of a 'club feel', where a majority of members have strong personal, business or social connections.

Director appointments in Ireland, particularly on publicly funded organisations or State boards, can be based on political and personal connections, creating the perception that due process has not been followed in such appointments. Board selection should be based on a rigorous selection process to ensure that the board has the best talent available and that appointments made are based purely on a candidate's skill set and relevant experience.

Women still find it difficult to become non-executive directors (NEDs) in Ireland because of this perceived 'clubiness' and the existence of a 'glass ceiling'.[2]

## Risk Management

### Key Failing

A key failing over the past 10 years has been the lack of effective risk management, for example in the financial services sector. This has resulted in failures where there was a chronic lack of understanding of the consequences of global systemic risk on the Irish financial system and Irish banks. Many institutions built loan portfolios that were heavily weighted to the property sector, which eventually became overheated and then collapsed.

---

[2] *Women on Boards in Ireland: Insights from women directors on the progress made and obstacles remaining* (Institute of Directors in Ireland, January 2013).

Many directors have lacked the necessary experience, insight and training to ensure that the executive management team identifies, addresses, monitors and manages the risks to which the company is exposed.

Increased regulatory requirements from the Central Bank of Ireland now require that credit institutions appoint a chief risk officer (CRO), with effect from 1 January 2015.

Despite the proactive approach taken by the Central Bank, managing the country's exposure to the financial services sector will always be difficult as inevitably markets will almost always be ahead of the regulation required, as businesses try to find jurisdictions with a light touch or simply no regulation.

## Non-Profits

While more commonly in the limelight, it is not just financial institutions that face high levels of risk. All organisations face challenges regarding their exposure to risks, be they operational, environmental, brand, technological, cyber, financial or competitive.

In 2012, 74% of non-profits in Ireland did not have a register of risks and only 17% had a disaster recovery plan, as suggested and outlined in several corporate governance reports.[3] All organisations need to address these issues or they may suffer as a result.

Recent revelations in relation to the Rehab Group[4] and the Central Remedial Clinic (CRC)[5] will also bring a greater focus on the responsibilities of the boards of non-profits. In addition, the governance requirements of non-profits will come under greater scrutiny due to the requirements of the new Charities Act (see **Chapter 1**).

## Compliance

Keeping up with the increasing number of regulatory requirements regarding risk and other issues, such as health & safety,

---

[3] For example, Grant Thornton, *Not-for-profit Survey 2012*.
[4] See "The €742,000 Cover-up: Secret deal for Ex-CRC chief", *Irish Independent*, 24 January 2014.
[5] See "Rehab used charity cash to pay for their staff cars", *Irish Independent*, 17 January 2014.

data protection, etc., is a key challenge for any organisation. Failure to meet these can result in penalties and negative publicity.

## Board Information

### Ensuring a Timely and Accurate Flow of Information

Perhaps the key factor in the success of any board is its ability to ensure that appropriate information is made available to it in a timely manner and in a form that is easily digested. Many boards fail this simple test.

A key challenge for a board is in ensuring that the executive management team provides it with accurate information, particularly when that information may be negative (for example, when sales are behind budget) or portray management in a bad light.

### Tone from the Top

The chair has a critical role in setting a 'tone from the top' that facilitates the timely flow of accurate and relevant information. This can be facilitated by promoting a culture of openness, constructive questioning, free debate and not 'killing the messenger'.

## Board Commitment

### Time Commitment

Aside from appointing the right people, boards face significant challenges in ensuring that all directors are able to commit the necessary time and effort to the business of the board.

If directors do not allocate sufficient time to prepare for meetings and familiarise themselves with the operations of the organisation, the board will be less effective and ultimately company performance will suffer.

Many directors underestimate the time commitment required of board and committee membership and as a result may treat board membership with less than the respect it deserves.

## Commitment to Governance Training

Governance training is typically the responsibility of the chair and the Company Secretary, who together ensure that it happens and is addressed on a regular basis.

## Board Productivity

### Size

The boards of many voluntary organisations, particularly in the education and healthcare sectors, and indeed some state-funded organisations, struggle to make effective decisions due to their size. Such boards can have memberships of over 30 people, which puts enormous constraints on its efficiency. While there is no 'right size' for a board, its size will be influenced by the size of the organisation, the range of skills and experience required to support it strategically, the stage of its development and the work to be carried out, either at board meetings or in committees. Larger boards tend to be less efficient. Consequently, smaller boards with the right composition tend to be more effective.

### Clarity of Focus

Those serving on boards may not always be clear about their duties, responsibilities and the commitment required. It is vital that the commitment required is clearly communicated as part of the recruitment process and covered off in an induction process. Importantly, the Charities Act 2009 and the Companies Bill 2012 spell out these duties and responsibilities specifically, which was not the case with previous legislation.

Board focus will be improved by having a clear strategy for the organisation, an annual business plan and risk assurance procedures in place. Without this, decision-making will take place in a vacuum.

### Workload Balance

A key challenge for any organisation is getting the balance of work right between the board, its committees and the executive management team. Planning the board agenda, i.e. the work of the board for the year, is a vital part of this.

## Board Atmosphere

The chair has an important role in creating the appropriate atmosphere in which board meetings are held. This should put existing and new board members at ease. This atmosphere should encourage openness, transparency, candour and constructive debate. An additional challenge for the chairperson and the nominations committee is in ensuring that board cliques or cabals do not emerge as these could obstruct the productivity of the board.

## Independent Challenge

The role of non-executive directors (NEDs) is to bring an independence of thought and objectivity to the boardroom. This valuable asset will assist the board to make tough or difficult decisions more efficiently. The quality of information available to NEDs is critical in this regard. If the information that the NEDs require is not made available, they should ask for it.

Board members should be able to challenge each other constructively and debate issues without letting personal agendas unduly influence future policy- or decision-making.

All of these challenges are closely linked. If qualified and competent directors are not on the board, it will struggle to make the right decisions on a timely basis.

This list is not exhaustive, but outlines some of the key challenges that face boards in Ireland today.

**Chapter 8** explores the future of corporate governance in Ireland and identifies specific areas to improve board performance.

# 3.

# Ethics and Values

- Definition
- The Importance of Ethics
- The Current Situation in Ireland
- Ethics and the Role of Boards
- Ethics in Practice
- Developing a Code of Business Ethics
- Conclusion

## Definition

*"Ethics is knowing the difference between what you have a right to do and what is right to do."*

Potter Stewart, US Supreme Court Justice

In a company context, business ethics provide guidelines for acceptable behaviour. Business ethics consist of deep-rooted values and principles that should directly influence both strategy and day-to-day operations. Values form the core of one's character and drive one's behaviour. Thus, values are the foundation stone for ethical business behaviour.

## The Importance of Ethics

The financial crisis prompted a renewed focus on ethical practices in business. Countless scandals in the banking sector, on publicly funded organisations (see **Appendix A7** for case studies on FÁS and Tallaght Hospital) and non-profits have left Ireland, and indeed many other countries, with a deep reputational crisis. Such failures stemmed from a mix of hubris, poor governance, pure greed and the absence of moral leadership. This has now led to greater public expectation that organisations will act in a more ethical and morally responsible way in the future.

Ethics and values are vitally important in setting the culture of an organisation and in shaping how it interacts with shareholders and stakeholders. It is now largely accepted that organisations have a responsibility not just to their shareholders but also to their stakeholders at large. These includes employees, customers, suppliers, competitors, local communities, the general public and the State.

Ethical behaviour is vital to organisations as it instils trust, empathy and builds reputation, which can in turn improve income, financial sustainability and widen the customer base.

However, while good behaviour breeds more good behaviour, the opposite is also true.

## The Current Situation in Ireland

In order to restore trust in Ireland and Irish business, a sharper and more ingrained focus on ethics and values is required. They are all interrelated.

Pressure from consumers, charitable donors, the State and the general public for greater transparency in relation to ethical business practices have seen many organisations choose to make a public commitment by developing codes of ethics, including stated principles such as honesty, integrity and fairness, and demonstrating that they are being implemented. In 2012, almost 70% of organisations had a business code of ethics in place.[1]

However, while codes of ethics can offer guidance for ethical behaviour, they are not prescriptive and are no substitute for identifying people of integrity to lead the organisation. Above all, ethics are about responsibility and leadership based on values appropriate to the organisation.

In Ireland, we need a cultural shift to repair our damaged reputation. This is happening, thankfully, but there is still some way to go. This change must start and be led from the top.

## Ethics and the Role of Boards

Boards, and in particular the chair, have a crucial role in establishing ethical standards and practices throughout an organisation. Good leaders will have an authentic and deep-rooted moral compass and will set the tone for ethical behaviour from the top of the organisation to the bottom.

Boards have the responsibility to set the company's values and standards and of ensuring that obligations to stakeholders are met. These board responsibilities include:

- agreeing and documenting the ethics and values of the organisation;
- as leaders, *living* these ethics and values;

---

[1] Chartered Accountants Ireland and Praesta Ireland, *The Art of Ethical Leadership* (2013).

- understanding the ethical issues that affect the organisation, its business or activities;
- supporting ethics programmes for staff;
- ensuring that the company can demonstrate that it lives up to its stated ethical values.

Board members should be given ethics training, which should also be provided for the whole organisation in turn. Compliance must be underscored by an ethical tone from the top, with strong board leadership and clear values. The induction process for all board members, as well as staff, is a great opportunity to introduce this.

When considering board appointments, board members should evaluate closely the values and integrity of any potential director in relation to those of the organisation. This should be done as part of the recruitment and interview process and is even more important when selecting the chair.

Boards will often face tough decisions when considering ethical problems. For example, maximising shareholder returns by paying taxes in overseas countries, rather than the home country, or using manufacturers in countries with questionable human rights records. If a board goes too far towards optimising profits, it could face reputational problems, as seen with several multinational companies (MNCs) in recent years. For example, Apple has been under the spotlight in the media for paying $36 million in corporation tax on sales of $7.11 billion in its Irish unit.[2]

Boards should also note that sometimes a decision that does not directly optimise profits is still in the company's broader and long-term interests for ethical reasons. For example, an investment by an Irish firm overseas may be enhanced through philanthropic investments in the local community, which may assist with earlier brand recognition. This will be at the expense of longer term profit, but should help the sustainability of the company in the region in the long run. Another example would be an energy company investing in plant the capital cost of which may impact short-term profits but which will reduce carbon emissions in densely populated areas and

[2] *The Irish Times*, 7 March 2014.

demonstrate the company's commitment to the surrounding community and customers.

## Ethics in Practice

Irish businesses should be paving the way in establishing good ethical practices. Under the EU green paper, *The EU corporate governance framework* (see **Chapter 1**), having a business ethics policy is regarded as a key component in corporate governance. Boards need to be aware of the ethical issues they face or could face and prepare accordingly.

Ethical issues can be encountered frequently in all types of organisation and can include:

- bribery and corruption;
- discrimination and bullying;
- inappropriate labour practices by third-party suppliers;
- safety and security;
- scope of personal data acquisition and storage;
- security of personal data;
- conflicts of interest.

All organisations should establish an ethics programme. Such a programme would include the following elements.

**A code of ethics:**

- A code of business ethics sets the foundation for ethical behaviour and is shaped by the values of the organisation. Codes should be reviewed every few years so that they remain relevant and practical. Sample outline contents for a code of business ethics (or 'conduct') are shown in **Appendix A6**. (Coca-Cola and the ESB in Ireland are examples of well thought through codes of business ethics.[3])
- Communication of the code of ethics is important. Some organisations include it in staff manuals or handbooks, others include it

---

[3] See http://www.esb.ie/main/about-esb/code-of-ethics.jsp and
http://www.coca-colacompany/investors/code-of-business-conduct

online or in the annual report or provide it as part of the recruit-ment and induction process.

**A continuous training agenda:**

- Training in ethical behaviour is crucial to ensuring all employees know what is expected of them; it helps instil the ethical culture of an organisation.
- Organisations should have an individual responsible for ethics. This will vary as to who takes this role, but it can be a member of staff within the CEO's office, legal, risk or another department.

**A means to report breaches of the code of ethics:**

- A means for raising ethical concerns should be provided.
- Organisations should encourage whistle-blowers and foster a culture whereby they are rewarded (and protected) for coming forward about unethical behaviour.

**Rewarding those who 'live the ethical culture':**

- Ethical behaviour should be recognised and rewarded.
- Likewise, those who breach the code of ethics should face disci-plinary action.
- Requirements to follow and conform to the code of ethics should also be included in employees' contracts.

**Monitoring and reporting:**

- Organisations should monitor the effects of their ethics programmes.
- Many organisations issue corporate social responsibility (CSR) reports annually, which will cover ethics and values.

## Developing a Code of Business Ethics

It is important that every organisation has a written code of business ethics to help guide the behaviours of its employees or members. Such a code communicates the organisation's values to employees, suppliers, customers, clients and the wider general public. Given the lack of focus on business ethics over the last decade, many customers and stakeholders now actively seek out firms that promise to do business in an honest and ethical manner.

For business leaders, developing a code of ethics is critical in setting the tone from the top of the organisation and the behaviours that it implies.

The key steps in developing a code of business ethics for an organisation are as follows:

- Identify and research sample codes of ethics from organisations in similar and comparable businesses or sectors. The code should fit the organisation – global multinational companies will have very different issues and therefore different codes of ethics compared to an SME enterprise trading in a local market. For example, the intercultural issues may be different.
- Examine those documents very carefully and look for themes that are relevant to your organisation. Look outside your industry and country to ensure best practice is captured and followed.
- In reviewing code of ethics/conduct that are relevant to your organisation, pay particular attention to how the organisation states its vision and mission and any specific policies new staff receive as part of their induction in this regard. These documents can include policies on taking gifts from suppliers, working from home, expense claims, paternity leave, behaviour at staff functions outside work, web and social media usage, etc. Review these documents to understand what behaviours and standards exist today in your company, which are good and positive and where the gaps are.
- In developing the code of ethics, think about the ethical dilemmas that face not only your organisation but also the wider industry or sector. These ethical issues vary by sector, and it is important to directly address them in the company's code of ethics. For example, a distributor in some Middle Eastern countries or in Africa is likely to have to bribe customers as a matter of course, as that is how business is done there. Capturing this issue in a code of ethics will be challenging.
- Ensure that you get input from employees and stakeholders when you create the code of ethics/conduct. Many organisations make the mistake of leaving staff 'out of the loop', but frontline employees frequently confront ethical dilemmas. Ask employees for specific examples of situations that have made them feel uneasy and where they need guidance and try to incorporate

those ideas into the draft code of ethics. Focus groups may also be helpful in discussing the code of ethics as it evolves.

- Address potential workplace issues, such as office relationships, in the code of ethics.
- Assign an individual or a task force in your organisation to take responsibility for developing the code of ethics and ensure they have the mandate and resources from the chair and/or the chief executive to carry out their work. It is essential in developing the code of ethics that the process is open and transparent and that everybody has the opportunity to contribute. Stakeholder engagement will be a critical part of this. The chair and chief executive is ultimately responsible for the content of the code of ethics and its implementation.
- Circulate the draft code of ethics to the board, to staff and to key stakeholders for comment before finalising it. Ensure that the code is reviewed from both a legal and 'plain English' perspective before it is implemented. A key challenge for the organisation will be ensuring it is kept alive and provides a moral compass in uncertain situations.

## Conclusion

Ethics and ethical decision-making should underline everything an organisation does. Recent scandals have highlighted the dangers and risks of not adhering to this approach.

Profit-making enterprises should take into account the impact of their actions on all stakeholders, not just shareholders.

For non-profit organisations, ethical behaviour is essential in upholding their integrity and accountability and is crucial to ensuring long-term trust.

For publicly funded bodies, anything other than the highest ethical standards and behaviour will undermine their purpose and prove highly detrimental if, for example, trust becomes an issue.

In order to restore Ireland's reputation, all organisations should examine their ethical practices and develop a code of business ethics that can be demonstrated to have made a difference operationally to the organisation on a day-to-day basis.

## CHECKLIST FOR CREATING AN ETHICAL CULTURE

- Do we have an established code of conduct?
- Does the board espouse our values and ethical behaviour?
- Do we offer regular, practical training in ethical practice?
- Do we have an external reporting mechanism for whistle-blowing?
- Do we enforce our ethical guidelines and take action accordingly?
- Are employees informed and aware of the ethical code?

# 4.

# Building Blocks of Corporate Governance

- Introduction
- The Chief Executive
- The Executive Management Team
- The Board of Directors
- The Chairman
- Non-executive Directors
- Executive Directors
- The Company Secretary
- Board Committees

## Introduction

Corporate governance is concerned with developing the appropriate structures and processes for directing and managing an organisation. The same corporate governance framework may not always be appropriate for all companies. For example, the stage of growth of a company, its strategic focus or geographical spread may influence the type of structures and processes it needs to put in place.[1]

A company in the early stages of growth will require very different structures from those of public limited companies (PLCs), which are required by the Irish Stock Exchange to comply with the *UK Corporate Governance Code*[2] combined with the "Irish Corporate Governance Annex", or a state organisation which must comply with the *Code of Practice for the Governance of State Bodies*.[3]

As a chairman or a director, it is important to have an informed view of the appropriate corporate governance framework required to support the organisation and its business strategy.

The building blocks of corporate governance are shown below in **Figure 1**.

The key building blocks of corporate governance are based on the following roles and groups:

- chief executive
- executive management team
- chairman
- board of directors
- non-executive directors
- executive directors
- Company Secretary
- board committees.

In this chapter, discussion on corporate governance matters will apply to all organisations unless the content applies specifically to companies.

---

[1] FRC, *The UK Corporate Governance Code* (2014).
[2] Irish Stock Exchange, *Main Securities Market Listing Rules and Admission to Trading Rules*, Appendix 4, "Irish Corporate Governance Annex" (ISE, 2011).
[3] Department of Finance, *Code of Practice for the Governance of State Bodies* (2009).

## FIGURE 1: THE CORPORATE GOVERNANCE FRAMEWORK

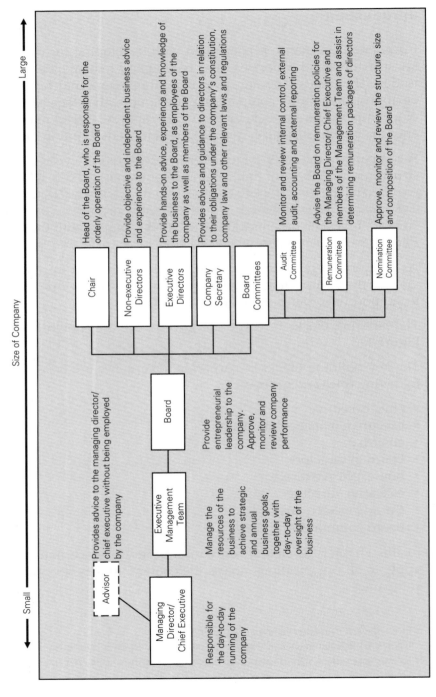

Small ————— Size of Company ————— Large

**Managing Director/ Chief Executive**

Responsible for the day-to-day running of the company

**Advisor**

Provides advice to the managing director/ chief executive without being employed by the company

**Executive Management Team**

Manage the resources of the business to achieve strategic and annual business goals, together with day-to-day oversight of the business

**Board**

Provide entrepreneurial leadership to the company. Approve, monitor and review company performance

**Chair**

Head of the Board, who is responsible for the orderly operation of the Board

**Non-executive Directors**

Provide objective and independent business advice and experience to the Board

**Executive Directors**

Provide hands-on advice, experience and knowledge of the business to the Board, as employees of the company as well as members of the Board

**Company Secretary**

Provides advice and guidance to directors in relation to their obligations under the company's constitution, company law and other relevant laws and regulations

**Board Committees**

**Audit Committee**

Monitor and review internal control, external audit, accounting and external reporting

**Remuneration Committee**

Advise the Board on remuneration policies for the Managing Director/ Chief Executive and members of the Management Team and assist in determining remuneration packages of directors

**Nomination Committee**

Approve, monitor and review the structure, size and composition of the Board

# THE CHIEF EXECUTIVE

The title 'chief executive' is often used instead of 'managing director', although in the case of a chief executive he or she may or may not be appointed to the board whereas a managing director will always be (see also below). For the sake of consistency the term 'chief executive' also means managing director, unless specified otherwise in this book.

The first building block of corporate governance to be put in place in the company/organisation is the chief executive. In start-ups the founder generally fills this position.

Whatever the size or nature of the company, the role of the chief executive is to ensure that the company achieves its strategic objectives and to provide leadership and direction to the executive management team and staff. His or her role depends on the stage of growth of the company. Typically, the scope of the role becomes more clearly defined as the company develops and the supporting corporate governance framework evolves. For example, once such a governance framework is developed, the chief executive may delegate some responsibilities to members of the executive management team.

## Role of the Chief Executive

- Develop and deliver on the company's strategic plan in the most effective and efficient manner.
- Accountable for the overall performance of the company and for the day-to-day running and management of the company's business, under delegated authority from the board.

## Responsibilities of the Chief Executive

- Develop and present the strategic and annual business plans to the board for approval.
- Implement the board's policies and strategies.
- Report to the board on progress against the strategic and annual business plans on a regular basis. (Typically, reporting against the

37

annual plan will be monthly, while reporting against the strategic plan will be less frequent, although it should be at least two or three times a year.)

- Ensure that the flow of information to the board is well presented, easily digestible, relevant, timely and accurate, and is sufficient for the board to perform their role.
- Manage the day-to-day operations of the company.
- Ensure that financial results, business strategies and targets are communicated to those who need to know.
- Monitor the financial and operating results against plans and budgets.
- Manage, motivate, develop and lead members of the executive management team.
- Manage resources efficiently and effectively to achieve the company's objectives.
- Chair executive management team meetings.
- Take a leadership role in establishing or developing the company's culture and values.
- Ensure that there is a fit between the ethics and values of the organisation, its strategy and the company's processes and structure (see also **Chapter 3**).
- Ensure that the appropriate internal audit processes and procedures are in place (in liaison with the head of internal audit and/or the external auditors, if a board audit committee is not in place).
- Develop and maintain an effective framework of internal controls over risk in relation to business activities and report to the board as appropriate.
- Develop processes to ensure that investment proposals are reviewed thoroughly, that risks are identified and steps taken to manage them.
- Ensure that there is a succession plan in place for the executive management team.

## Advisors to the Chief Executive

In the early stages of a company's existence the chief executive may consult an advisor, who will typically be an external professional with the appropriate experience to assist in the development of the company and its governance structures. The role of the advisor may be one of mentor, coach, confidante, business advisor, etc. No matter what it involves, the nature and scope of such a role should be committed to paper so that there is absolute clarity on what it involves. By doing this, it is less likely that the advisor will be perceived as a shadow director. A shadow director is a person upon whose direction and instruction the directors of a company are accustomed to act.

## Shadow Directors

Section 27 of the Companies Act 1990 defines a 'shadow director' as a person upon whose direction and instruction the directors are accustomed to act. A person will not be regarded as being a shadow director if the directors follow advice given by such a person where they are acting in a professional advisory capacity.

Shadow directors are not formally appointed as directors. In addition, a person classified as a shadow director does not necessarily declare himself or herself as a director.

## Other Considerations

- The board can appoint a managing director from among its members and can delegate to such appointee any powers exercisable by the board. The board can also appoint a chief executive who may not be a member of the board. The managing director/chief executive is, in effect, delegated authority to manage and take decisions on the day-to-day running of the company.
- The duties, powers and remuneration of the managing director/chief executive are not fixed by law, but are entirely at the discretion of the board and can be amended or withdrawn by the board at will. Where the board wishes to use the term 'chief executive' or indeed wishes to appoint a chief executive who is not on the board, the company's Articles of Association should reflect this.
- The managing director (and in the case of a chief executive who *is* a director) is both an officer and an employee of the company.

- Best practice suggests that the role of the chairman and chief executive should be clearly separated. The *UK Corporate Governance Code,* which covers listed companies, specifies that the role of the chairman and the chief executive should not be exercised by the same person
- If the chief executive is also a member of the board, the legal implications outlined in the section below on "Key Legal Considerations for the Board of Directors" need to be considered.

## 10 QUESTIONS MOST LIKELY TO BE ASKED BY A BOARD OF THE CHIEF EXECUTIVE

1. What are the critical challenges facing the organisation in the coming months/year?
2. What is your biggest worry about the business?
3. How is the company performing against its strategic plan, its annual business plan budget and its competitors?
4. Have the company's resources been managed and deployed in the best way possible to achieve its objectives?
5. What contingency plans have been prepared to cope with unexpected events? Is there a risk management plan?
6. What are the most critical performance criteria for staff?
   (a) How are the key executives performing?
   (b) How do you assess and manage the performance of those who report to you?
7. Who would succeed/stand in for you if you were not available for whatever reason?
8. Is the board providing sufficient support and value to you and your team?
9. How are you conveying the company's ethics and values to staff?
10. What new skills/experience would you like to see on the board in the future?

### 10 Questions a Potential Chief Executive should ask before Accepting Appointment to the Position

1. Why am I being asked to consider this position?
2. Do I have the necessary skills and experience to fill this position?
3. Do I believe and therefore support **the mission, vision and strategic objectives of the company**?
4. What are the key issues facing the company?
5. What are the key risks and what processes are in place to deal with them?
6. What is the financial status of the company? What are the key messages from the management accounts, internal and external audit reports?
7. What skills and experience are available in the executive management team and are they appropriate to support the ambitions of the company?
8. Do I envisage having a good relationship with the current chairman of the board?
9. How does the board interact with the management team? Is there a good relationship in place?
10. Are the necessary resources available to enable the company to achieve its ambitions?

## THE EXECUTIVE MANAGEMENT TEAM

As a company grows, the chief executive may allocate specific areas of responsibility, such as finance, human resources, ICT, operations, etc. to individuals in the company. As these responsibilities become increasingly important, it is good practice to formalise these roles in writing in employment contracts, which will include the job descriptions.

Establishing an executive management team may be justified if the size of the company warrants it. Once established, the team provides clarity in relation to who does what and ensures accountability for each individual's responsibilities.

The functions typically assigned to individuals on the executive management team are:

- sales
- marketing
- operations/production/business units
- finance
- human resources
- risk and compliance
- information communications technology (ICT)
- company secretarial.

Some individuals may have responsibility for more than one area, depending on the size of the company.

## Role of the Executive Management Team

- Assist the chief executive to manage the resources of the organisation to achieve its strategic and annual business goals.
- Manage the day-to-day operations of the business.

## Responsibilities of the Executive Management Team

- Develop and manage the implementation of the strategic and annual business plans.
- Identify and address key strategic and business issues, and communicate these to the board.
- Manage the annual budgeting process.
- Regularly monitor and report on performance against strategic targets and the annual business plan.
- Develop a risk management strategy, address and manage the key risks and report to the board as appropriate.
- Play a key role in leadership and motivation of staff in the organisation and build upon the ethical foundations set by the board and the chief executive.

- Implement recommendations by the internal audit function and the external auditors that have been approved by the board of directors/audit committee, as appropriate.
- Meet as an executive management team on a monthly basis, or more frequently as required.
- Meet with the board at least twice a year to review in depth the strategic direction of the company.
- Communicate strategic, annual plans and company policy to ensure that everyone involved is working towards the same goals.
- Manage the operation and development of the function(s) for which the executive management team have individual responsibility.
- Provide accurate, appropriate and timely management information to the board, including high quality leading and lagging indicators in order to facilitate effective decision-making and measure progress. Leading indicators (e.g. inquiries, orders booked, sales pipeline) and lagging indicators (e.g. sales invoiced, cash balances, staff turnover) are used to judge the health of the business.

(See **Appendix A4** for Sample Terms of Reference for an Executive Management Committee.)

## Executive Management Teams: Insights and Practical Suggestions

- The number of members on an executive management team will depend on the size of the company. Generally, to be effective, it should not exceed six to eight people. Otherwise the CEO will find it difficult to give the time each of his direct reports merits to do their job successfully.
- The executive management team is typically made up of:
  - the chief executive;
  - heads of operations, production, business units, etc.;
  - heads of support functions, e.g. IT, finance, HR.
- Members of the executive management team who are not on the board may attend board meetings, when requested, to discuss specific issues.
- When the executive management team makes a collective decision, it must be supported by all members of the team, even if they do not agree with it, as once a decision is made it will have to

be supported outside the executive management room by all on the basis of collective responsibility.
- It is vital that the decision-making authority of the board and that of the executive management team is understood so that the 'line in the sand' between the two is clear.
- The executive management team and the board should participate in an 'away day' to discuss the strategic direction of the company and to build and foster relationships. These should happen once or twice a year.
- The executive management team must ensure that information regarding company performance in relation to finance, operations, marketing, HR, risk, health & safety and compliance is effectively communicated to the board at the level of detail required. Too often, only financial information is transmitted to the board, leaving gaps in the board's knowledge of other important areas of the business.
- There should be a formal performance management system in place to evaluate the performance of the executive management team. The performance of the CEO will be evaluated by the board or remuneration committee, if there is one.

(See **Appendix A4** for Sample Terms of Reference for a Remuneration Committee.)

## Key Legal Considerations for the Executive Management Team

Members of the executive management team may also be on the board as executive directors. The legal considerations identified in the section below, "Key Legal Considerations for the Board of Directors", would then apply.

### 10 QUESTIONS A CHIEF EXECUTIVE SHOULD ASK THE EXECUTIVE MANAGEMENT TEAM

1. Is the role of the board, executive management team and that of each of its members clear to everyone on the executive management team?

2. Are the existing management processes effective and efficient, and if not, how could they be improved?
3. Do we spend enough time on the issues that are critical to the company's success, e.g. profitability, cost control, people, customer service, funding?
4. Do we have the right information to manage the business?
5. Am I, as the chief executive, making the best use of the talent around the executive management table?
6. Are we providing appropriate leadership to the rest of the company?
7. Are the goals we are setting ourselves as a team ambitious enough, but yet realistic?
8. How can we get better value from the talent and experience around the boardroom table?
9. What is the most critical risk we have to manage to achieve our objectives for the year?
10. How can we demonstrate that we are actively living our ethics and values?

## THE BOARD OF DIRECTORS

Many of the failures during the current economic crisis have come about as a result of board and leadership failures in many sectors of the economy. Consequently, boards have come under increased scrutiny in recent years and the standards now expected of them have risen exponentially.

A company usually decides to establish a board of directors in order to:

- provide a greater degree of formality and rigour to the running of the company for the benefit of investors, staff, customers, government and other stakeholders;
- provide access to independent and objective external advice;
- utilise the experience and knowledge of non-executive directors (NEDs). For example, if a company needs to raise capital to fund expansion, it would be helpful to have somebody on the board with this experience;

- assist the growth of the company and bring on board NEDs with experience of joint ventures, key markets, etc.;
- raise the profile and status of the company.

Establishing a formal board requires careful consideration, since it can be difficult to reverse the decision because in doing so it may have an adverse impact on the company and the individual reputations of those concerned, if not handled appropriately.

The implications of having a formal board need to be considered. For example, the appointment of a board means there will be a greater degree of formality in place in the company and this may result in greater attention to detail and a longer decision-making process. However, it should also add to the quality of those decisions.

The appointment of a board, with the appropriate skills and expertise, should enhance the performance of the organisation.

## Role of the Board of Directors

- Provide "entrepreneurial leadership for the company, within a framework of prudent and effective controls, which enables risk to be assessed and managed".[4]
- Set and uphold the company's values, culture and ethical standards.
- Approve, monitor and review the company's strategic and business performance.
- Ensure the long-term success of the company.
- Protect and represent the interests of shareholders and other stakeholders as a whole.
- Act in whatever way they consider to be the best interests of the company.

## Responsibilities of the Board of Directors

- Set the strategic direction and objectives of the company, ensuring that the financial and other resources are in place to achieve them.
- Review, approve and monitor the strategic and annual business plans on an ongoing basis.

[4] FRC, *Guidance on Board Effectiveness* (March 2011).

- Review company performance against targets, including bench-marking against the competition.
- Ensure that the executive team consistently adheres to and implements policy and procedure as advised.
- Monitor legal, ethical, risk and environmental compliance.
- Determine the nature and extent of significant risks the board is willing to take and maintain sound risk management and internal control systems.
- Allocate responsibility for specific tasks to board members, such as being a member of one of the board's committees (see **Appendix A4** for Sample Terms of Reference for Board Committees).
- Draw up a schedule of matters specifically reserved to the board for decision, e.g.:
  - issue of new capital
  - borrowings
  - acquisitions and divestments
  - dividend policy
  - remuneration of non-executive directors. The remuneration committee (made up of NEDs) is responsible for the remuneration of executive directors and the chairman. Remuneration of NEDs is a matter for the board or, if required by the Articles, the shareholders.
- Appoint and/or remove the chief executive and plan for orderly succession.
- Oversee the review of the performance of the executive management team and its individual members.
- Hire, advise, compensate and, if necessary, remove members of the executive management team.
- Outline in the annual report the general policy for board renewal and re-election.
- Include a Directors' Compliance Statement in the annual report, if required. Under the new Companies Act this will apply to all Plcs, whether listed or not, and to all private companies whose turnover exceeds €15.23 million or whose balance sheet exceeds €7.6 million. This statement will report on compliance with the company's relevant obligations, including:
  - company law
  - tax law

> ○ any other obligation that provides a legal framework within which the company operates and that may materially affect the company's financial statements.

- Ensure that the company's financial statements are audited in accordance with accepted accounting standards and policies.
- Approve the financial statements for each accounting period, which give a true and fair view of the state of affairs of the company.
- Hold an annual general meeting to communicate with company shareholders.
- Hold board meetings on a regular basis. The number of board meetings will depend on the workload of the board, the number of committees, the size and complexity of the company. Six to eight meetings per year would be normal.
- Meet with the executive management team as a whole at least once a year to review the strategic direction of the company.
- Undertake a rigorous and formal evaluation of the board's own performance and that of individual directors at least every two years.
- Share responsibility for board decisions (whether present at the board meeting or not). *Note*: as individuals, directors have no specific powers to make decisions or take actions on their own. Decisions are those of the *board*.
- Ensure there is a healthy and constructive relationship between the board, the chief executive and the executive management team.

(See **Appendix A3** for a sample schedule of Matters Reserved for the Board. These are decisions that can only be made by the board as they are above the authority limit of the executive management team. Examples would be capital expenditure and acquisitions.)

## Boards of Directors: Insights and Practical Suggestions

In this section we outline the attributes and elements of what makes successful boards.

### *What Makes Boards Successful*

- The success of a board of directors will depend on the personalities involved and how well they work with each other. Often the decision to join the board of a company is influenced by the names of those already on the board, their reputation and whether one knows them or not. However, potential directors should always carry out their own due diligence.

- Successful boards will have the right mix of skills and experience to support the strategic direction of the company.
- Terms of reference for the board should be drawn up and agreed upon by the entire board to ensure there is clarity of understanding on its role for all concerned. (See **Appendix A4**, Sample Terms of Reference for Board Committees.)
- The board is constantly evolving to support the future direction of the business. It is typically the role of the nomination committee to ensure that board renewal is constantly on the agenda and that succession is carefully planned.
- Directors who serve on too many boards will dilute the contribution they can make to any one individual board.
  - The *UK Corporate Governance Code* directs that the board should not agree to a full-time executive director taking on more than one non-executive directorship in a FTSE 100 company nor the chairmanship of such a company.
  - The Irish Central Bank guidelines have set a limit in relation to directorships at credit institutions and insurance undertakings. For major institutions, a director can hold the following directorships without requiring the prior approval of the Central Bank:
    - up to three financial directorships; and
    - up to five non-financial directorships.
- For a non-major institution, a director can hold the following directorships without requiring the prior approval of the Central Bank:
  - up to five financial directorships (i.e. directorships in companies or groups of companies which are credit institutions or insurance undertakings); and
  - up to eight non-financial directorships (i.e. any other type of company which is not a credit institution or an insurance undertaking).
- The Health Information and Quality Authority's Report on Tallaght Hospital suggested that a board of a hospital should

have no more than 12 members.[5] (See **Appendix A8** for a case study on Tallaght Hospital.)

- Although the board is responsible for ensuring that the executive management team runs the company efficiently, it should not become overly involved in the running of the company except when serious operational issues arise.
- Visibility of board members around the organisation builds up the credibility of the board and will help board members to learn more about the company.
- The board should ensure that the executive management team considers the key risks to which the business is exposed and puts in place a plan of action to address them.
- The manner in which non-executive members of the board challenge the executive members is important for board harmony. For example, if the questioning is inappropriate, executive directors can build up a resistance to the non-executive directors which can be to the detriment of board effectiveness. However, the chair should always encourage board members to constructively challenge, where appropriate.
- The boardroom should not necessarily be a place of comfort; challenge, along with teamwork, is an essential feature of board life.
- Lunch or dinner after a board meeting provides a good opportunity to build relationships among board members who may not otherwise meet in a more informal setting.
- A significant proportion of executive directors' remuneration should be structured so as to link rewards to both corporate and individual performance.
- There should be a transparent remuneration policy and clear procedures and no director should be involved in deciding their own remuneration.
- Directors should receive induction on joining the board and should regularly update their skills and knowledge, which should be facilitated by the Company Secretary.

---

[5] *Report of the investigation into the quality, safety and governance of the care provided by the Adelaide and Meath Hospital, Dublin, incorporating the National Children's Hospital (AMNCH) for patients who require acute admission* (HIQA, 8 May 2012).

## *Board Representation*

- The board can be made up of a number of:
  - ○ executive directors (see the section on Executive Directors below), representing the executive management team and providing in-depth knowledge of day-to-day operations; and/or
  - ○ non-executive directors (see the section on Non-executive Directors below), bringing an independent and challenging perspective and enhancing the decision-making process.
- A balance should exist between the number of executive directors and non-executive directors, so that no individual or group of individuals can dominate the board. There are differing views as to the appropriate balance of executive directors and non-executive directors, but best practice indicates that NEDs should be in the majority.
- According to the *UK Corporate Governance Code*, except for smaller companies, at least half of the board (excluding the chair) in a listed company should be comprised of non-executive directors who are considered independent, and an explanation given where this is not adhered to. (A 'smaller company' is one that is outside the FTSE 350 throughout the year immediately prior to the reporting year.)
- In the case of smaller listed companies, at least two non-executive directors are recommended.
- The "Irish Corporate Governance Annex" requires that an explanation be given in the annual report of the company as to why the number of NEDs is regarded as sufficient, the process involved in their selection, factors considered when determining their independence and a description of their skills and experience.
- The board should consist of members with diverse but appropriate experience and knowledge of the sector and with a balance of skills to support the strategic objectives of the company.
- The board should identify in the annual report each non-executive director it deems to be independent and whether there are circumstances or relationships likely to affect their judgement.
- In the absence of a nomination committee, the chief executive and chairperson must work together with the board in deciding on an appropriate recruitment process for directors.

## Chief Executive and Executive Management Team Succession

- Primary responsibility for succession planning at executive management team level lies with the board, with input from the chief executive where appropriate.
- The board is responsible (whether by itself or on a recommendation from the nomination committee) for orderly succession, for appointments not only to the board but also for the chief executive and for the executive management team.
- The circumstances surrounding the retirement of the chief executive will determine whether he or she may have a role in the process for selecting a successor.

## Board Meetings

- The chairperson, chief executive and the Company Secretary should communicate in advance of board meetings to discuss the agenda and any issues of concern. In some organisations the chairperson, chief executive and Company Secretary hold an agenda meeting a number of weeks or so in advance of the board meeting to decide on the agenda and to plan for the meeting. Advance circulation of the agenda and information (at least a week in advance of the meeting) is best practice to enable board members to be well prepared for the meeting.
- The number of board meetings required will depend on the stability of the business, the volatility of the market(s) in which it operates, the amount of work to be carried out and the confidence of the board in the experience and skills of the executive management team.
- Board meetings should be held for a length of time that ensures meaningful engagement takes place. Ideally, they should not last for more than three hours, except in extenuating circumstances, which will occur from time to time.
- With regard to board committees, such as the audit, nomination or remuneration committees, no-one other than the committee chairman and committee members are entitled to be present at these meetings, but others may attend at the invitation of the relevant committee.

- According to the Irish Central Bank's *Corporate Governance Code for Credit Institutions and Insurance Undertakings,* 'major institutions' must hold board meetings at least 11 times per year, one per calendar month.

## Key Legal Considerations for the Board of Directors

### *Directors' Duties*

- Directors are required to act in the best interest of the company. They have a wide range of both statutory and non-statutory duties.
- The Companies Acts impose a number of duties and liabilities on directors; for example, the Companies Bill 2012 (which at the time of writing is expected to be signed into law in late 2014 and commenced in 2015) provides that it is the duty of each director of a company to ensure that the company complies with the requirements of the Companies Acts.
- Under the new Companies Bill, single director companies will be permitted once a separate Company Secretary is appointed. Previously, a company had to have two directors. The Company Secretary role can be outsourced to a third party.
- Directors also owe a number of other fiduciary duties to the company in respect of which they are appointed. These duties have been codified under the Companies Bill 2012 into eight main duties, including a duty to:
  - act in good faith in what the director considers to be the company's interests;
  - act honestly and responsibly in relation to the conduct of the affairs of the company;
  - act in accordance with the company's constitution (which will replace the current Memorandum and Articles of Association) and to exercise his or her powers only for purposes allowed by law;
  - not to use company's property, information or opportunities for his or her own or others' use unless approved by the members or the company's constitution;
  - not to fetter discretion unless permitted by the company's constitution or entered into in the company's interests;

- o avoid conflicts of interest unless agreed by members of the company or by the company's constitution;
  - o exercise care, skill and diligence; and
  - o have regard to the interests of the company members as well as employees.
- While directors are required, in the performance of their functions, to have regard to the interests of the company's employees in general as well as the interests of its members, their prime duty is owed to the company alone. In recent times, case law has seen this expanded to provide for directors owing duties to creditors in the case of insolvent companies.
- Directors of certain companies will be required under the new Companies Act to prepare a **compliance statement** (which is to be included in the Directors' Report filed with the annual accounts) regarding the company's policy on compliance with relevant obligations, such as provisions of the Companies Act, tax law, etc.
- The directors must also set out in the compliance statement the procedures that have been put in place within the company to ensure compliance with relevant obligations and the arrangements for implementing and reviewing the effectiveness of these policies and procedures, or must explain why this is not the case. Relevant obligations are those obligations under the Companies Acts where failure to comply would constitute a Category 1 or Category 2 offence (i.e. the most serious offences), a serious market abuse offence or a serious prospectus offence, and also include obligations under tax law.
- The directors' compliance statement must be in writing, approved by the board, reviewed and, if necessary, revised at least once in every three-year period. The company's external auditors will also be required to assess the fairness and reasonableness of this statement.

## *Directors' and Officers' Liabilities*

Directors' liabilities have increased significantly in the last 10 years or so because of the increase in statutory duties and the cumulative effect of court decisions. Consequently, many directors are concerned at the impact of this personal liability if claims are brought against them for poor management of company affairs. In certain circumstances, such as insolvency, a director's liability may be unlimited. The degree of liability will depend on the background and experience of the director and what that director should have done in certain circumstances. The courts may take a different view on director liability depending on the background of the director and what he or she should have known. For example, with regard to a financial issue, a chartered accountant may be treated differently from someone with a HR background. The extent of liability will also be dependent on whether the directors are NEDs or executive directors. Consequently, it is vital that each director is very clear about what his or her duties are.

A director may also be liable to third parties in certain circumstances where he or she is personally responsible for a particular contract. If the company's insurance is inadequate to cover a specific loss, then the director, if he or she can be linked to the loss by the plaintiff, could be personally liable for damages. Consequently, it is critical that the company has the appropriate insurance cover in place for all eventualities.

Directors may also have liabilities to staff who not only sue the company but may also sue the director personally, for example for harassment.

## Directors' and Officers' (D&O) Insurance

Directors' and officers' (D&O) insurance offers protection for directors and officers of companies against claims arising in the performance of their business duties.

A D&O policy provides insurance against executive malpractice, responding to allegations of 'wrongful acts' brought against the directors and officers of a company. A 'wrongful act' is usually defined as a breach of duty, neglect, misstatement, error and omission by directors or officers while acting in their capacity as such.

In light of recent events in financial services, in particular, directors and officers are exposed to potentially greater risks of litigation due to lower investor tolerance for performance and governance failures. If they lack sufficient D&O coverage, directors and officers will be dependent on their organisation's ability to protect them if they are held liable. However, due to the increased severity of claims, directors and officers face a greater risk because companies (particularly small and medium-sized enterprises) may not be able to protect them financially from the large costs involved in today's litigation. The *UK Corporate Governance Code* provides that listed companies should arrange appropriate insurance cover in respect of legal action against their directors.

There are a wide variety of D&O policies available. Directors should evaluate the cover provided by various insurers and should understand what is covered and, more particularly, what is *not* covered before committing to a policy. In addition to understanding the policy, directors should understand how it relates to them on joining, serving and leaving a company. It will be important to understand the implications for director and officer insurance cover if directors do not leave in good standing.

D&O insurance has become a highly technical area and relevant advice should be sought before taking out such a policy.

## 10 QUESTIONS AN INDIVIDUAL SHOULD ASK BEFORE ACCEPTING A NON-EXECUTIVE DIRECTORSHIP

1. What do I need to know about the company and its industry?
   - Strategic plan
   - Company's marketplace and competitive position
   - Developing trends and related forecasts
   - Regulations governing the industry
   - Accounting and reporting methods used within the industry
   - Risks within the industry.
2. How has the company performed over the last three years and what are its plans for the future?
3. Can I speak to previous members of the board to ensure that I understand the ethics, values and culture of the organisation and to ensure that they are in line with my own?
4. What is the company's record in relation to corporate governance?
5. What are the competencies, capabilities and weaknesses of the board, and how can I complement them?

6. Why, specifically, am I being asked to join the board and can I add value to the company?
7. What time commitment will the position require and can I meet it?
8. What risks am I potentially exposing myself to?
9. What information do I need to satisfy myself that this organisation is being properly managed, e.g. management accounts, internal audit reports, external audit post-audit memos, staff turnover, legal cases, risk management reports, etc.
10. How are the members of the board and executive management team perceived by the business community?

## 10 QUESTIONS TO BE CONSIDERED BY THE BOARD IN RECRUITING A DIRECTOR

1. Will our process for recruiting new board members attract the best candidate?
2. What information do we need to provide to encourage non-executive directors to consider joining? This could include the strategic plan, codes of governance, etc.
3. Does the board search process consider relevant diversity needs, such as gender, race or ethnicity?
4. What skills and experience should we be seeking to recruit to complement those we already have on the board?
5. Can the board target any strategic needs that could be addressed through greater diversity? Diversity could mean gender, nationality, experience, etc.
6. Can we give the candidate exposure to several of our current directors for informal discussion, both to gain a variety of views on the candidate and to let the prospective director judge the 'chemistry' of the board?
7. What will be the internal and external perception of the proposed candidate?
8. Can the individual commit the necessary time to the board?

> 9. Does the proposed director have the necessary skills, expertise and experience to fulfil their role on the board?
> 10. Is the proposed director a candidate for chairperson in the future?

## THE CHAIRMAN

The *UK Corporate Governance Code* provides that an independent, non-executive director should chair the board. Furthermore:

> "The roles of chairman and chief executive should not be exercised by the same individual. The division of responsibilities between the chairman and chief executive should be clearly established, set out in writing and agreed by the board."[6]

The appointment of a non-executive chairman of the board is an important step in improving corporate governance in companies. As a result, the chief executive will become more accountable to the board than may have been the case in the past.

The chairman plays a crucial role in any organisation in setting the ethical tone and in establishing the company's corporate governance.

There will be a number of reasons why a company appoints an independent, non-executive chairperson. These may include:

- gaining from the person's experience in chairing and managing boards elsewhere;
- gaining from specific expertise that the chairman might have, e.g. expertise of the financial markets or the cultures of similar organisations;
- providing greater investor and stakeholder confidence;
- being part of a more rigorous approach to corporate governance;
- increasing the profile of the company and attracting better candidates for the board.

---

[6] *UK Corporate Governance Code* (FRC, 2014), para. A.2.1.

It is the chairman's responsibility to drive the development of the corporate governance in the company.

## Role of the Chairman

- The chairman is responsible for the leadership of the board and ensuring its effectiveness in all aspects of its role.
- Ensure that the company achieves a satisfactory return on investment for its shareholders.
- Set and maintain the highest standards of integrity and probity, set clear expectations concerning the company's culture, values and behaviours and the style and tone of board discussions.
- Oversee the orderly operation of the board of directors.
- Ensure appropriate interaction between the board, its shareholders and executive management.

## Responsibilities of the Chairperson

- Chair board and shareholder meetings.
- Serve as the company's primary representative to key external and internal stakeholder groups. (This responsibility could be shared with the chief executive.)
- Take a leading role in determining and reviewing the composition, structure and performance of the board.
- Ensure that the board determines the nature and extent of the significant risks that the company is willing to embrace.
- Ensure that the company has a risk management plan that is reported against on a regular basis.
- Foster a good relationship of mutual trust with the chief executive and develop strong working relationships with all executive directors and the rest of the executive management team.
- Ensure that decisions are reached in the best interests of the company.
- Ensure that the board undertakes a thorough analysis of all issues and concerns.
- Ensure that board committees are properly established and operated with appropriate terms of reference (see **Appendix A4**, Sample Terms of Reference for Board Committees).

- Exploit board members' knowledge and experience and ensure that all board members contribute during meetings.
- Ensure that the company has a strategic plan, supported by an annual business plan and budget.
- Ensure that all members of the board have access to accurate, timely and clear information.
- Put in place the appropriate plans to facilitate succession of the chief executive.
- Develop agendas for board meetings for the year in consultation with the chief executive and the Company Secretary (see the section below on the Company Secretary).
- Ensure that a process is put in place to assess the performance of the board.
- Ensure that the board is up to date with relevant corporate governance issues.
- Create the appropriate environment to foster constructive debate and effective decision-making by the board.

## Insights and Practical Suggestions: The Chairman

The key challenge for the chairman is to ensure that the company gets the maximum possible benefit from its board. There are a number of ways to improve board effectiveness, such as by:

- providing timely, accurate and relevant information to enable board members to perform their role;
- fostering a spirit of openness and honesty around the boardroom table;
- acknowledging the input of board members;
- making it clear to the chief executive that he or she is accountable for company performance;
- maintaining contact with board members to source informal feedback on board performance and critical issues;
- ensuring that the company has the appropriate corporate governance structures in place;
- obtaining expert opinion where necessary.

An important role of the chairman is to ensure that cliques do not develop among board members. Once these develop, they can be very difficult to break up.

Overly dominant directors can impact negatively on the performance of the board and executive management team, so the chair will need to be able to manage these.

The chairman must be supportive of the chief executive and work at building a collaborative relationship.

If relationships between the chief executive and members of the board impact the productivity of board meetings, then the chairman should bring this to the attention of the chief executive to discuss the cause of such issues and possible solutions.

The board should consider the appointment of one of the independent non-executive directors to be the senior independent director. A senior independent director is a director who does not have a material interest in the company and does not own shares. Their only interest in the company will be in receiving fees for being a director. He or she should be available to shareholders where concerns are not met by the chairman or the chief executive (see "The Senior Independent Director Role" below).

The chairman should meet with the chief executive a week before each board meeting to discuss any issues on the agenda or that are likely to arise.

The chairman should arrange to meet with executive and non-executive directors individually, for example over dinner, to build relationships.

## Key Legal Considerations for the Chairman

- The chairman's role is of obvious importance. Not only is he or she responsible for ensuring that order is preserved at board and other statutory meetings, such as the AGM and an EGM, but also (with the assistance of the Company Secretary) that such meetings are conducted in a proper manner having regard to law and the rules of the organisation in question. Procedural propriety is important to ensure that the validity of the meeting and the resolutions passed cannot be questioned.
- Under the Irish Central Bank's *Corporate Governance Code for Credit Institutions and Insurance Undertakings*, the chairman must be a non-executive director and must be put up for re-election

annually. He or she must also demonstrate that he or she can commit the required time to the role.

- The chief executive of a credit institution cannot advance to the role of chairman of that institution within five years of leaving the post of chief executive of that institution. The chairman cannot hold the position of chairman or chief executive of more than one credit institution or insurance undertaking at any one time.

### 10 QUESTIONS A CHAIRMAN MAY ASK THE CHIEF EXECUTIVE

1. How satisfied are you with the performance of your executive management team?
2. If we were starting the company again tomorrow, would you hire them all?
3. How can we make better use of board time?
4. Are you satisfied with the input and value you get from the board?
5. How can we improve company governance?
6. Do we have the right skills and competencies on the board to deliver on the strategic plan?
7. How can we provide the board with the comfort that the risk management plan is realistic? What evidence can we provide to support this?
8. What is the biggest risk facing the company and is it being managed effectively?
9. If you were to get more time with the board (e.g. at an offsite meeting), how should you spend it?
10. How can we improve the way we work together?

## NON-EXECUTIVE DIRECTORS

As the company develops, additional skills may be required to support its strategy. For example, the company may be looking to expand into a different country or acquire certain types of companies. The appointment of non-executive directors (NEDs) with these particular skills to the board can help to achieve the company's strategy.

As with the appointment of a chairman, the appointment of a NED means that the chief executive will be answerable to a greater number of people with differing skills and experience. Consequently, this should improve overall company performance.

NEDs can play a key role in the governance of a company by bringing an outsider's independent and objective perspective. Therefore, they can make a considerable contribution to the development and success of a company.

Before considering the appointment of a NED, it is critical that the role they are being asked to perform is clearly thought through and communicated to them for consideration. This will be the role of the board and also the nomination committee (see section on '**Board Committees**' below).

NEDs may also be appointed to the board for other reasons. If funds are being provided by a venture capital company, the provision of funding may be contingent on a representative being appointed to the board. This often results in greater accountability for shareholder funds and improved company performance.

## The Role of Non-executive Directors

The role of non-executive directors is to provide objective and independent advice to the board to enable it to make better decisions in the interest of all shareholders and stakeholders.

## Responsibilities of Non-executive Directors

- Bring a genuine independent and external perspective to stimulate board debate and enhance decision-making.
- Provide value-added input to strategy and strategic development.
- Act in the best interests of the company as a whole rather than any one particular group of shareholders.
- Assist in carrying out the duties of the board, such as:

- o reviewing, approving and ongoing monitoring of the strategic plan;
- o reviewing organisational capability in relation to stated objectives;
- o reviewing financial performance against targets;
- o raising capital;
- o reviewing any major changes in the company, such as the financial and organisation structure;
- o providing advice on major investments/divestments to be made;
- o monitoring legal, ethical, risk and environmental compliance where appropriate.
- Act as a catalyst for change and challenge the status quo, when appropriate.
- Maintain the highest ethical standards, probity and integrity of the company.
- Ensure that financial controls and systems of risk management are robust and operating effectively.
- Monitor and constructively challenge the performance of the executive management team.
- Assess and assist the executive management team to address and manage risk.
- Play a lead role in the nomination, remuneration, audit and risk board committees (see section on **'Board Committees'** below).
- Play an active role in assisting the chief executive in the replacement of key senior management and in planning for management development and succession.
- Attend board committee meetings, as appropriate. (A NED may also have special responsibility for audit, nomination and/or remuneration committees.)
- Attend board meetings, ad hoc meetings with the chairman and meetings of non-executive directors, as appropriate.
- Ensure that the financial information is accurate, timely and clear, and that financial controls and systems of risk management are robust and defensible.
- Maintain the confidentiality of information received.
- Carry out functions with due skill, care and diligence.
- Devote sufficient time to their responsibilities.
- Undergo specific and relevant training for the role.

# Insights and Practical Suggestions: Non-executive Directors

## *Independence of Non-executive Directors*

- Ideally, non-executive directors should be financially independent, in the sense of not having to rely on the company for a major part of their income. This ensures that a NED does not have to consider the personal financial consequences of his or her independent advice if it is rejected by the board for whatever reason.
- Shareholding by NEDs is a contentious issue as it may not be compatible with complete independence. However, there may be circumstances where a reward of equity or share options is appropriate. This will be a matter for the remuneration committee.
- NEDs should have the blend of experience, independence and objectivity that is best suited to the particular strategic requirements of the company and the role they have been selected for.
- With regard to credit institutions, the Central Bank's *Code* requires boards to assess the employment experience, business relationships, directorships and objectivity of potential non-executive directors, to ensure there is no conflict of interest.

## *Appointing Non-executive Directors*

- In both public and private companies, it is usual for the Articles of Association to provide that directors are appointed by the company at an annual general meeting. Under the Articles, directors can also typically under the Articles be co-opted in the interim to fill casual vacancies until the next AGM, at which stage a decision is made by the members as to whether such a person should continue as a director. The appointment of a director under the Companies Bill 2012 is similar.
- It is the responsibility of the chairman and the board, in the absence of a nomination committee, to lead the process for the appointment of both executive directors and NEDs to the board, subject to the approval of the members at general meetings. The chief executive may have input into this process.

- Appointing former executive directors as NEDs requires careful consideration. It is often regarded as a questionable practice as it is unlikely that they would be regarded as independent or indeed objective.
- New or prospective NEDs should speak to previous NEDs of the company before taking up their positions in order to get an insight into how the business functions, the firm's culture, etc.

## Number of Non-executive Directors

- The size, complexity and nature of the company's business will have an influence on the number of NEDs serving on the board.
- Under its *Corporate Governance Code for Credit Institutions and Insurance Undertakings*, the Central Bank of Ireland requires there to be a minimum of two NEDs on the boards of financial institutions.
- It is important to have an adequate number of NEDs on a board and to have fresh blood coming in on a periodic basis. The number of NEDs should outnumber the executives on the board to avoid the 'forcing through' of proposals from executive directors under a vote. If this happens on a regular basis, the composition of the board should be reviewed.
- It is better to have at least two NEDs on a board rather than only one, as otherwise it will be a lonely position. Two NEDs are much more likely to be effective in challenging the board.
- According to the *UK Corporate Governance Code*, at least half of the board (excluding the chairman) in a listed company should be comprised of NEDs. The "Irish Corporate Governance Annex" indicates that where this is not complied with, a reasonable explanation should be given.
- In the case of smaller listed companies, two independent NEDs are recommended.

## The Senior Independent Director Role

As indicated above, there may be a role for a senior independent non-executive director to:

- assess the performance of the board and the chairman, and hold meetings of the NEDs privately;

- be available to shareholders if they believe their concerns are not being resolved through the normal channels of chairman or chief executive, or if such contact is not appropriate;
- act as the voice of the non-executive directors;
- act as the 'conscience of the board';
- act as a sounding board for the chairman and as an intermediary for the other directors;
- work with the chairman, shareholders and other directors to resolve issues in a time of crisis;
- intervene if there is a dispute between the chairman and the chief executive.

## Non-executive Directors' Terms of Office

- The term or terms a NED serves on the board may vary depending on the company, but they should be appointed for a defined period.
- It is recommended that two terms of three years should be considered, with a possible extension for a further three years.
- The reappointment of NEDs should not be automatic and should be subject to appointment at the AGM.
- In determining their term(s) of office, the following should be considered:
  - the period should be sufficiently long enough for the NEDs to be of benefit to the company, particularly if it is a complex business;
  - the period should not be so long that it compromises the ability of the NEDs to be independent and objective.

## Induction

Induction is the process by which new directors are introduced into a company:

- An individual appointed to the board should undergo a comprehensive, tailored induction programme on the responsibilities of directors. This should include visiting facilities, understanding the business strategy, the strategic planning process and being introduced to senior staff. Good induction will accelerate the contribution that a new NED can make to the board and the company.

- Subsequent, follow-up training should be provided for all directors, particularly in relation to new laws and regulations. Directors should keep abreast of developments within the company, its sector and the legal, regulatory and governance environment.

## *Other Considerations*

- An adequate time commitment is necessary if an effective contribution is to be made by a NED to the board. Today, the role of a NED is much more time-consuming than in the past. NEDs have much more responsibility as there tends to be a greater focus on them if things go wrong.
- NEDs should insist on receiving high-quality information sufficiently in advance of meetings to enable them to perform their role.
- It is important to keep in mind that although companies may try their best to keep NEDs as well informed as possible, the reality is that the executive directors will always be more knowledgeable about the company's internal operations and therefore it may be difficult to challenge them on matters of detail.
- If listed on a stock exchange, NEDs should be familiar with the major stock analysts who cover the industry and the company.
- NEDs should be familiar with the largest shareholders/ stakeholders, their interests, politics and priorities. Stakeholders could include community groups, employees, local authorities, etc.
- If necessary, the chairman and the NEDs could meet outside of board meetings to discuss matters that cannot be discussed in front of executive board members.
- NEDs should undertake their own due diligence to satisfy themselves that the company is one in which they have confidence and to which they can make a valuable contribution.

## Key Legal Considerations for Non-executive Directors

- Irish company law does not distinguish between the responsibilities of executive directors and non-executive directors (NEDs). The term 'non-executive' director is understood in practice to mean a director who is not an employee of the company and

is, therefore, not directly involved in its day-to-day management. He or she is only required to dedicate part of his or her
time to the company's affairs. NEDs participate fully in board
deliberations, but have no executive function in the company's
management.
- The same legal duties and obligations apply to all directors,
although the courts may apply different standards when determining the level of skill and standard of care that a NED can be
expected to demonstrate.
- Company directors' responsibilities are wide and diverse. Their
duties arise primarily from two sources: statute (Acts of the
Oireachtas and other legislation, e.g. EU legislation) and
common law.

## Directors' Common Law Duties

Directors' common law duties can be summarised under three
principles:

1. Directors must exercise their powers in good faith and in the
interests of the company as a whole.
2. Directors are not allowed to make an undisclosed profit from
their position as directors and must account for any such profit.
3. Directors are obliged to carry out their functions with due care,
skill and diligence.

## Directors' Statutory Duties

A director's **statutory duties** as a company officer under the Companies Acts 1963–2013 are as follows:

- duty to maintain proper books of account
- duty to prepare annual accounts
- duty to have an annual audit performed
- duty to maintain certain registers and other documents
- duty to file certain documents with the registrar of companies
- duty of disclosure of certain personal information
- duty to convene general meetings of the company
- duties regarding transactions with the company
- duties of directors of companies in liquidation and directors of
insolvent companies.

## *Directors' Duties under New Companies Act*

As discussed in **Chapter 1** above, Chapter 5, section 228 of the Companies Bill 2012 sets out directors' duties comprehensively, consolidating statutory and common law duties. The key innovation is the codification of directors' fiduciary duties into eight duties, which shall be owed to the company.

### DIRECTORS' DUTIES UNDER THE COMPANIES BILL 2012

A director shall:

1. act in good faith in what the director (subjectively) considers to be the interests of the company;
2. act honestly and responsibly in relation to the conduct of the affairs of the company;
3. act in accordance with the company's constitution and exercise his or her powers only for the purposes allowed by law;
4. not use the company's property, information or opportunities for his or her own or anyone else's benefit unless this is expressly permitted by the constitution or approved by resolution of the members in general meeting;
5. not agree to restrict the director's power to exercise an independent judgment unless this is expressly permitted by the company's constitution or the director believes in good faith that it is in the interests of the company to fetter his or her discretion in relation to a particular transaction;
6. avoid any conflict between the director's duties to the company and his or her other (including personal) interests, unless the director is released from this duty in accordance with the constitution or by a resolution of the members;
7. exercise the care, skill and diligence which would be exercised in the same circumstances by a reasonable person having both the knowledge and experience that may reasonably be expected of a person in the same position as the director and the knowledge and experience which the director has;
8. in addition to the general duty owed to employees, have regard to the interests of the company's members (i.e. the owners of the company).

In addition to the above, directors will have a general duty to ensure that the company complies with the Companies Act. Furthermore, on agreeing to act as a director they must acknowledge in writing the duties and obligations imposed on them by companies legislation, other legislation and the common law.

Directors will also have other specific responsibilities, such as:

- ensuring that the Company Secretary has the necessary skills to maintain the appropriate records;
- where they are likely to be in a contract or proposed contract with the company, that they declare the interest at a directors' meeting or to the chair, if a meeting is not going to take place in time. If the contract is in the normal course of trade, this is unlikely to be an issue; it is only an issue if there is likely to be a conflict of interest;
- for certain types of company, it is necessary to include a directors' compliance statement in the directors' report or explain why they have not (see the discussion on the Companies Bill 2012 above, where this is discussed in more detail).

The Bill makes clear that the duties above shall be owed not only by persons formally appointed as directors of a company but also by shadow directors and de facto directors (i.e. persons who occupy the position of director despite not having been formally appointed as such).

## EXECUTIVE DIRECTORS

Members of the executive management team may be appointed to the board once they are considered to be a driving force within the company and key to its strategic development. This is an extremely important decision. As with all other appointments, once executed, they are difficult to reverse. Executive directors should only be appointed to the board if they are leading drivers of growth and influence in the company.

When deciding on whether to appoint an executive director to the board, the board needs to identify the specific benefits of that appointment, given that the board can always ask members of the executive management team to attend board meetings, as and when required.

Therefore, the key question to be asked is: what added value will the new executive director bring to the board?

Executive directors must overcome any conflict of interest they have by being on the board while also being on the executive management team and implementing the board's policies. While on the board they must prioritise the interests of the company as a whole and not their individual executive interests.

## Role of the Executive Director

It is an executive director's role to provide independent, objective advice and the benefit of their day-to-day experience to enable better decisions to be made in the strategic interests of the company.

## Responsibilities of an Executive Director

- Support the chief executive in the management of the company.
- Provide first-hand, in-depth knowledge of the organisation.
- Act in the best interests of the company as a whole even when this might conflict with their role as a member of the executive management team.
- Be fully informed with regard to all issues relevant to the work of the board.
- Participate in board meetings and decision-making.
- Ensure that company compliance and risk management policies are being maintained.
- Remain detached from considerations of self-interest.
- Challenge opinions and constructively criticise the work of colleagues on the board.
- Maintain the confidentiality of information received.
- Carry out functions with due skill, care and diligence.
- Participate in the day-to-day management of the organisation.
- Insist on receiving full, accurate and timely information from the executive management team, even if this may reflect poorly on their role on the executive management team.

## Insights and Practical Suggestions: Executive Directors

### *Attributes of a Potential Executive Director*

There are a number of desirable attributes for a potential executive director to have:

- comprehensive understanding of the company and its industry/sector;
- specific management and functional expertise;
- proven past success;
- particular knowledge and experience that would be valued by the board;
- capacity as a strategic thinker and change agent;
- objectivity and integrity;
- excellent communication and decision-making skills;
- ability to demonstrate independence in role on the board.

Additionally, an executive director can be a potential successor to the chief executive.

Executive directors should have a significant personal stake in the long-term success of the company to ensure responsible action on behalf of shareholders and other stakeholders. *Note:* executive directors are not on the board for their independence, unlike NEDs.

## Induction of Executive Directors to the Board

An individual appointed to the board should receive the same induction as a non-executive director. Subsequent training should be provided, particularly in relation to new laws and regulations.

## Other Considerations

- Executive directors are primarily involved in the running of the company. It can be difficult for them, as directors on the board, to extract themselves from their business responsibilities and govern with an adequate degree of independence and objectivity.

- They must, therefore, ensure clarity of purpose in their dual role on the executive management team and the board. While on the board they must act in the best interests of the company as a whole.
- The chairman should respect reporting lines when resolving issues with executive directors.
- The chairman should create an environment where executive directors are comfortable challenging their executive colleagues, although this would be best done at executive management team meetings beforehand to avoid any disharmony.

## Key Legal Considerations for Executive Directors

- The term 'executive director' is not statutorily defined. It is understood in practice as meaning a director who is an employee of the company and is, therefore, directly involved in its day-to-day management. An executive director will be required to dedicate almost all, or at least a substantial part of, his or her time and attention to performing his or her role within the company, whereas a NED is likely to be on other boards.
- Importantly, an 'executive director' has the same responsibilities under the law as a non-executive director.

### 10 QUESTIONS A BOARD SHOULD CONSIDER BEFORE APPOINTING AN EXECUTIVE DIRECTOR

1. What added value could the individual contribute that cannot be gained by his or her attendance at the board meeting in a management capacity?
2. Would this appointment to the board enhance this individual's contribution to the company?
3. What has been the quality of the individual's contributions to the board to date?
4. How will the individual's skills complement those of the existing board members?
5. Does the individual have a clear strategic perspective on the future direction for the company?

6. How is the individual regarded by the members of the board and the executive management team at present?
7. What is the working relationship between the individual and the chief executive?
8. What is the relationship between the individual and the existing NEDs?
9. If this person were made a director, how would it be perceived externally?
10. If this individual is not appointed to the board, what are the potential implications?

## THE COMPANY SECRETARY

Under Irish company law, the Company Secretary is appointed by the board and can only be removed by the board. They will only be a member of the board if they are a director or a non-executive director.

The position of Company Secretary is a very important one as he or she is responsible for supporting the board and the governance process, providing advice and guidance to the board on company law and regulations, its own policies and best practice in corporate governance.

Due to the increasing importance of corporate governance, particularly since the global financial crisis, there has been increased focus on the role of the Company Secretary. Given the growing complexity of this area, it is essential that the person responsible is given every opportunity to keep up to date on all relevant governance matters.

### The Role of the Company Secretary

- Provide advice and guidance to the board of directors on their obligations under the company's Memorandum and Articles of Association,[7] company law and other relevant laws and regulations.

[7] These documents will be replaced by the company's "constitution" under the new Companies Act.

- Oversee the company's day-to-day administration and ensure specifically that the company complies with the law and observes its own rules and policies.
- Act as the principal legal and compliance (including corporate governance) officer.

## Responsibilities of the Company Secretary

The responsibilities of the Company Secretary are laid down in the Companies Acts 1963–2013. The Companies Bill 2012 states that the duties of the Company Secretary shall, without derogating from the Secretary's statutory duties and other legal duties, be such duties as are delegated to the Secretary, from time to time, by the board of directors of the company.

These may be supplemented by other functions set out in the Articles of Association of a company, in addition to further duties, which the directors may bestow upon the Company Secretary. The precise role of the Company Secretary is not, however, clearly defined and may vary greatly from one company to the next.

### *Statutory Duties of the Company Secretary*

The Company Secretary has important statutory duties, which will likely include:

- maintaining the company's registers, including those of the members, the directors and secretaries and the interests of the directors and secretaries;
- arranging annual and extraordinary general meetings of the company and circulating members with the documents for those meetings;
- organising meetings of the board and sub-committees of the board and ensuring that the directors have the papers they need to consider the issues that are to be discussed;
- preparing the minutes of company general meetings and meetings of the board and its sub-committees;
- making the company's registers, minute book and other similar documents available for inspection by the board and the public, where appropriate;

- sending updated information and documents on time to the Companies Registration Office (CRO) and to other regulatory bodies;
- publishing legal notices in the media;
- keeping custody of the company seal; and
- providing the directors with legal and administrative support.

## Other Duties of the Company Secretary

- Ensure that the company's corporate governance arrangements are in place, well documented and communicated to the organisation.
- Review periodically if these governance procedures and systems are effective and consider any necessary improvements.
- Ensure that board members receive high quality, relevant and up-to-date information in advance of meetings to enable them to perform their role.
- Attend meetings of the board, shareholders and board committees, and assist with drafting of the agendas, minutes, etc.
- Be familiar with company's procedures around board meetings.
- Act as a confidential sounding board to the chairman, non-executive directors and executive directors.
- Act as a link between the board and the executive management team, and help management understand the expectations and value sought by the board.
- Ensure that the company holds the AGM within the time limits specified.
- Keep the board informed of any new legislation that is applicable to them.
- Organise and administer board meetings. These responsibilities include:
  - notifying directors of the time, date and place of the board meeting, in good time;
  - preparing an agenda in liaison with the chairman;
  - ensuring that the agenda is accompanied by all documents that need to be considered by the board in advance of such meetings;
  - ensuring that any registers that need to be inspected by the board are available;
  - making the minutes available to the auditors.

- Communicate, where appropriate, outcome of board deliberations throughout the organisation.

## Insights and Practical Suggestions: The Company Secretary

- While much of the Company Secretary's role is administrative as opposed to managerial, the function of this officer is important given his or her extensive duties and responsibilities. Best practice has seen the importance and scope of this role increase in recent years. The Secretary now plays a key role in keeping the company's corporate governance structures up to date in liaison with the chairman.
- The new Companies Bill imposes a duty on the company to make sure that the Secretary has the necessary skills to discharge his or her statutory and other legal duties. The Company Secretary must, under the Companies Bill, give a declaration acknowledging that he or she has legal duties and obligations imposed by the Companies Acts and other statutes, and common law.
- As the Companies Bill outlines several different types of company, the Secretary should consider these different types and decide which one would best suit his or her existing company's activities.
- The Company Secretary needs to be an effective and involved participant at board meetings and should be included in informal functions outside the boardroom. At the same time, it must be made clear that he or she has no deliberation or decision-making function or vote on board matters if he or she is not a director.
- The Company Secretary can add value by anticipating the introduction of new regulations and briefing the board on the potential implications.
- The Company Secretary should not be a member of the executive management team if at all possible. However, this will depend on the size of the company.

## Key Legal Considerations: The Company Secretary

- The Company Secretary owes the company duties of skill, care and diligence in carrying out his or her role and can be liable in negligence for failing to carry out the role to the appropriate standard.

- In a public limited company (unlike in private companies), a certain level of skill and expertise is statutorily required by those who fill the office of Company Secretary (section 236 of the Companies Act 1990).
- Generally speaking, for all types of company, the Company Secretary is required to keep a register of members, minutes of meetings, directors and Secretary, declarations and notices of interest, directors' and secretary's interests, debenture holders, interest in shares and debentures and of beneficial interests in shares.
- As an officer of the company, the Company Secretary can be liable to be penalised as being an 'officer in default' where the company defaults in the duties that are imposed on it under the Companies Acts.
- Personal liability can be imposed upon the Company Secretary in a number of situations under the Companies Acts. This includes where a Company Secretary is concerned with fraudulent or reckless trading or where the company fails to keep proper books of account.
- As the legal and compliance officer, the Company Secretary should procedurally ensure, along with the chairman, that board and other company meetings are conducted in a proper manner, having regard to the law and the rules of the body in question. Procedural propriety is important to ensure that the validity of the meeting and the resolutions passed cannot be questioned

## 10 QUESTIONS TO HELP IMPROVE THE EFFECTIVENESS OF THE COMPANY SECRETARY

1. How much time does your Company Secretary allot to board-specific matters? Is it enough time to perform the role?
2. Does your Company Secretary regularly update the board on the latest corporate governance issues (changes in the law, investors' concerns, better board organisational ideas, etc.)?

3. Does the Company Secretary have a regularly updated record of each board member's telephone numbers, e-mail address and contact information?
4. Does the board make best use of the Company Secretary's office in preparing for annual meetings?
5. As part of the board's evaluation programme, do members examine ways in which they could make the Company Secretary's board duties easier? Should your Company Secretary also have an input in evaluating the board?
6. In an emergency, how quickly would the Company Secretary be able to contact a quorum of board members to decide on urgent matters? (A 'quorum' is the minimum number of board members required to have a validly constituted board meeting, which is normally set at two.)
7. Have the Chair and Company Secretary discussed needs and issues in the preparation of board meeting information and minutes?
8. Does your board know the process by which the Company Secretary assembles board mailings? Does either side see any problems with the current system that they could help address?
9. Is the Company Secretary exploring ways to save money on board operations or improve efficiency (use of telephonic/ video conference meetings or communication technology to dispatch meeting notices/agendas, savings on travel or accommodation, etc.)?
10. Does the Company Secretary's office benchmark other company secretarial functions for best practice on board support and governance duties?

# BOARD COMMITTEES

Board committees are established when the size or complexity of the company merits it.

Establishing a board committee enables board members to explore areas of particular sensitivity or difficulty in greater detail than may be possible at board level. Board committees are established to deal with specific duties of the board, such as audit, nomination and remuneration. Other board committees may be put in place depending on the nature of the business. For example, if a company is involved in a large number of acquisitions, there may be a need to appoint a board committee which addresses this area.

Board committees are only composed of board members, although they may invite outsiders to attend for the purpose of assisting the meeting. The board, in establishing a board committee, should set out the powers, duties and responsibilities (the **terms of reference**) of that committee.

In this section we describe the role of the:

- Audit Committee
- Nomination Committee
- Remuneration Committee
- Risk Committee.

All board committees should have written terms of reference that clearly outline their role (see **Appendix A4** for Sample Terms of Reference for each of the above committees).

## The Audit Committee

### Role of the Audit Committee

Monitor and review internal controls, external audit, financial controls, accounting and external reporting.

### Main Responsibilities of the Audit Committee

- Report to the board on all matters covered by its terms of reference and how it has discharged its responsibilities.
- Monitor the integrity of the financial statements of the company and any formal announcements relating to the company's financial performance, and review significant financial reporting issues contained therein.
- Review the company's internal financial controls and risk management systems, unless these are addressed by another board committee.

- Monitor and review the effectiveness of the company's internal audit function.
- Approve the appointment or removal of the head of the internal audit function, where it exists, or an outsourced internal audit function.
- Review major audit issues and accounting policies.
- Review the content of the annual report and accounts and advise the board on whether they are fair, balanced and understandable, and provide adequate information for the shareholders.
- Review company compliance with ethical standards, regulations, policies and practice reviews.
- Act as the link between the board and the external auditors.
- Review and monitor the external auditor's independence, objectivity and effectiveness of the audit process, taking into account professional and regulatory requirements.
- Monitor the supply of non-audit services by the external auditors, taking into account relevant ethical guidance regarding the provision of non-audit services by an external audit firm.
- Make recommendations to the board to be put to the shareholders for their approval in relation to the appointment of the external auditor and to approve his or her remuneration and terms of engagement.
- Meet with the external auditors twice a year, once at the planning stage and once post-audit at reporting stage.

(See **Appendix A4** for Sample Terms of Reference for an Audit Committee.)

## Insights and Practical Suggestions: Audit Committees

- The audit committee should be provided with sufficient resources to undertake its duties.
- Non-executive directors (NEDs) on the audit committee should meet the external auditors at least annually without the presence of any executive board members.
- The chair of the audit committee should attend the AGM.
- Audit committee membership should consist of a minimum of three independent NEDs of the board, at least one of whom must have recent and relevant financial experience. Two NEDs are recommended for smaller companies. It is desirable that at least one

member should have a professional qualification from one of the professional accountancy bodies, such as Chartered Accountants Ireland.

- The audit committee chairman should not be the chairman of the board.
- An audit committee may be an unnecessary overhead for smaller companies. If this is the case, a board member may be given responsibility for performing the internal audit function. Small companies could outsource their internal audit requirements.
- An audit committee meeting should be held at least annually and at such other times as the chair of the committee shall require.
- An audit committee should have access to the services of the Company Secretary on all committee matters.
- The audit committee should have written terms of reference that provide a clear understanding of its role and these should be tailored to the particular company.
- A separate section of the annual report should outline how the committee has discharged its responsibilities.
- For listed companies and financial institutions, the committee must be composed entirely of NEDs, the majority being independent.
- If a company has changed its business model to be more competitive during the economic crisis, there is a higher likelihood that its financial statements will need more careful analysis to ensure the appropriate accounting policies have been identified and applied.
- An audit committee should seek reassurance that the auditors and their staff have no financial, business, employment or personal relationship with the company that could adversely affect the auditor's independence and objectivity.

## Key Legal Considerations: Audit Committees

- The *UK Corporate Governance Code* specifies that all PLCs should have an audit committee comprising at least three NEDs. At least one member of the committee should have recent and relevant financial experience.
- Section 42 of the Companies Act 2003 requires that all Irish-registered PLCs, whether listed or not, establish and adequately resource an audit committee.

- Private companies limited by shares with balance sheets exceeding a total of €25 million or turnover greater than €50 million, in both the most recent financial year of the company and the year immediately preceding, also fall within the ambit of section 42 of the 2003 Act.

### 10 QUESTIONS TO HELP IMPROVE THE EFFECTIVENESS OF THE AUDIT COMMITTEE

1. How detailed are your audit committee's terms of reference? Do they spell out:
   - an itemised yearly schedule for the committee?
   - all the documentation the committee should see?
   - the committee's stand on key accounting principles and standards?
2. What specific qualifications and background (if any) do you require for the audit committee chair?
3. Does the company actively support continuing education requirements for audit committee members, utilising the company's internal audit staff or outside audit resources?
4. How regularly is the audit committee in touch with internal company officers, such as internal audit and the director of finance/chief financial officer, and how thorough are reports from these officers?
5. What is the audit committee's role in reviewing funding and liquidity issues?
6. What specific financial details are most crucial to your business sector, strategic targets and company structure? How can the committee give these more attention?
7. Does the audit committee meet privately with the external auditor, and how substantive are these discussions? What is your external auditor's personal view of the company's internal control systems?
8. Ask the company/external audit staff to 'audit' your committee in light of Stock Exchange/SEC policy changes discussed above. How will you be affected?

9. How involved is your audit committee in selecting and negotiating with the external audit firm?
10. Has the audit committee compiled its separate section of the annual report, relating to its specific issues, performance and effectiveness?

## The Remuneration Committee

### *Role of the Remuneration Committee*

Advise the board on the remuneration policies for the chief executive, the chairman, executive directors, the Company Secretary and the other members of the executive management team it is designated to consider.

### *Responsibilities of the Remuneration Committee*

- Determine and agree with the board the framework or broad policy for the remuneration of the chief executive, chairman, the Company Secretary and such other members of executive management as are designated to the committee. The remuneration of NEDs shall be a matter for the chairman and the chief executive. No director or executive manager should be involved in any decisions as to their own remuneration.
- In determining such policy, the remuneration committee takes into account all factors that it deems necessary. The objective of such policy should be to ensure that members of the executive management team of the company are provided with appropriate incentives to encourage enhanced performance and are, in a fair and responsible manner, rewarded for their individual contributions to the success of the business.
- Review the ongoing appropriateness and relevance of the remuneration policy.
- Approve the design of, and determine targets for, any performance-related pay schemes operated by the company and approve the total annual payments made under such schemes.

- Review the design of all share incentive plans for approval by the board and shareholders.
- Determine the policy for, and scope of, pension arrangements for the chief executive and other senior management (as determined by the board).
- Ensure that contractual terms on termination, and any payments made, are fair to the individual and the company, that failure is not rewarded and that the duty to mitigate loss is fully recognised by the company.
- Within the terms of the agreed policy, determine the remuneration packages of the chairman, chief executive and the executive management team, including salary, bonuses, pension rights, incentive payments and share options. The committee may/shall consult the chief executive about proposals relating to the remuneration of senior management.
- Oversee any major changes in employee benefits structures throughout the company.
- Be exclusively responsible for selecting (including setting the criteria), appointing and setting the terms of reference for any remuneration consultants who advise the committee.
- Make available the committee's terms of reference – these should set out the committee's delegated responsibilities and be reviewed and, where necessary, updated annually.
- Report the frequency of and attendance by members at remuneration committee meetings in the annual report.

(See **Appendix A4** for Sample Terms of Reference for a Remuneration Committee.)

## Insights and Practical Suggestions: Remuneration Committees

- As stated above, but it bears repeating, no director or executive manager should be involved in any decisions relating to his or her remuneration.
- The remuneration committee should have written terms of reference drawn up by the board, which provide a clear understanding of its role.
- Remuneration committee membership should, in listed companies, consist of at least three (or in the case of smaller companies,

two) independent non-executive directors (NEDs) of the board, each of whom shall be appointed by the board.[8]

- Where possible, particularly in financial institutions, all members of the remuneration committee will be NEDs.
- The chair of the remuneration committee is appointed by the board and should be an independent NED. Under the *UK Corporate Governance Code*[9] the chairman of the board is not eligible for this position, but in smaller listed companies he or she may perform this role.
- The remuneration committee should make its terms of reference available to all shareholders, explaining the role and authority given to it by the board.
- The chair of the remuneration committee should attend the company's AGM.
- The remuneration committee should meet at least once a year.
- The committee should benchmark the compensation packages of the company against comparator companies. However, they should use such comparisons with caution and relate increases in pay, etc. to improvements in performance.
- The committee should be sensitive to pay and employment conditions at the level below the executive management team in the company to ensure that any policies are justifiable and can be defended.
- The remuneration committee should consult the chairman of the board and chief executive about remuneration proposals for executive directors.

### 10 Questions to Help Improve the Effectiveness of the Remuneration Committee

1. How independent are the directors on the remuneration committee? Aside from their independence from the company, do they have any personal or business links with the chief executive?

---

[8] *UK Corporate Governance Code* (FRC, 2014).
[9] *Ibid.*

2. What performance measures do the company's pay incentives actually reward (return on investment, share price appreciation, earnings, strategic milestones achieved, etc.)? What other measures or KPIs were considered, and why were the ones used by the remuneration committee selected?

3. If you graph chief executive rewards along with your chosen measures of corporate results over the past few years, do they closely follow one another? If not, why not?

4. What is the average yearly time commitment required for service on the remuneration committee? Can it manage all the pay issues in the time available?

5. Does the remuneration committee have the authority and budget to hire outside consulting resources of its own?

6. Has the remuneration committee set share ownership targets for executive managers (or for the board itself)?

7. How fully does the remuneration committee review pay and incentive packages for members of the executive management team?

8. Are there 'unconventional' perks that could be offered to the chief executive or other executives that might cost less overall but prove more valued?

9. Is the remuneration policy for directors and the board reviewed frequently and tied closely to performance?

10. Does the remuneration policy reward long-term growth and profitability over short-term improvement?

## The Nomination Committee

### Role of the Nomination Committee

The role of the nomination committee is to assess the director requirements of the board going forward. This will include:

- monitor, review and evaluate the structure, size and composition of the board;

- identify new skills and experience requirements;
- plan for orderly rotation of directors;
- lead the process for all board appointments (executive, non-executive and the chairman), and make recommendations to the board in this regard.

## Responsibilities of the Nomination Committee

- Review the structure, size and composition of the board and make recommendations to the board.
- Ensure the board and its committees have the appropriate balance of skills, experience, independence and knowledge to achieve its strategic goals and discharge its duties effectively.
- Identify and nominate candidates to fill board vacancies when required. The board will subsequently review and approve the nominations, as appropriate.
- Give full consideration to succession planning for directors and other senior executives.
- Ensure that appointments to the board display the appropriate degree of diversity of gender, backgrounds, skills, social connections and nationalities necessary.
- Prepare a description of roles and capabilities for particular appointments.
- Assess the time commitments of each board position and ensure that the individual candidates have sufficient available time to undertake them.
- Ensure that on appointment to the board, NEDs receive a formal letter of appointment setting out clearly what is expected of them in their role.
- NEDs should be appointed for specific terms, subject to re-election and to any statutory provisions relating to the removal of a director. Any term beyond six years for a NED should be rigorously reviewed.
- Assess the leadership needs of the company in terms of its ability to compete in its industry/sector.

(See **Appendix A4** for Sample Terms of Reference for a Nomination Committee.)

## Insights and Practical Suggestions: Nomination Committees

- Nomination committee membership should consist of a majority of independent NEDs. While a committee of three members is usually recommended, companies with larger boards could consider increasing this number to four or even five members.
- A NED should chair the nomination committee. (The chairman of the board can also be chair of this committee provided he or she does not chair the discussion on his or her successor.)
- The nomination committee should normally meet twice a year.
- The chairman of the nomination committee should ensure that he or she attends the company's AGM.
- Non-listed (especially smaller non-listed) companies often will not have a nomination committee. In such cases, it is usual (whether or not in the context of a formal committee) for the chairman of the board and a NED to lead the nomination process, with active involvement from the chief executive, following which the board will make the final decision as to board appointments.
- The nomination committee should have written terms of reference that provide a clear understanding of its role.

### 10 QUESTIONS TO HELP IMPROVE THE EFFECTIVENESS OF THE NOMINATION COMMITTEE

1. Have the terms of reference been agreed with the board?
2. Does the company have a clear idea of the roles currently being played by each of the directors on the board? If not, why not?
3. Do the roles played by the existing directors clearly support the achievement of the business strategy?
4. What new talent is required to support the business strategy?
5. When do the terms of office of the existing directors come to an end? Does the company have a view as to whether any particular term or terms of office should be renewed or not?

6. If the company does not have a view, what information is required in order to establish that view?
7. What search process and selection process should be used to find new director talent?
8. Has the company ensured that any appointments to the board display a degree of diversity with regards to their personal connections to the company, gender, skills and knowledge?
9. What information is required about the company to show to potential directors, e.g. company strategy, performance, governance arrangements, profile of the management team, etc.?
10. What do we need to do to give potential directors a feeling for the culture of the organisation?

## The Risk Committee

### Role of the Risk Committee

The risk committee, where in existence, is separate to the audit committee in that it provides oversight and advice to the board on the current risk exposures and future risk strategy of the company.

### Responsibilities of the Risk Committee

- Assess and estimate the likely impact of the full range of risks to which the organisation is exposed, including financial, operational, commercial, reputational, data loss, cyber, brand, legal, safety and environmental risks.
- Advise the board on risk appetite and tolerance for future strategy, taking account of the board's overall risk appetite, the current financial position of the institution and its capacity to manage and control risks.
- Communicate regularly with the board in relation to ongoing risk assessment and advise them on the effectiveness of strategies and policies in place.

- Ensure the ongoing maintenance of risk management and reporting systems.
- Consult external experts where necessary, depending on the industry and risk exposure.
- Ensure compliance with any regulatory requirements in relation to risk, for example the requirements of the *Corporate Governance Code for Credit Institutions and Insurance Undertakings*.
- Ensure that there is a crisis management plan in place.

(See **Appendix A4** for Sample Terms of Reference for a Risk Committee.)

## *Insights and Practical Suggestions: Risk Committees*

- A risk committee is a requirement for financial institutions and insurance undertakings in Ireland under the Central Bank's *Corporate Governance Code for Credit Institutions and Insurance Undertakings*.
- Best practice has also seen an increasing number of companies adopt both audit and separate risk committees. This will depend on the scale of the company.
- The committee should have an appropriate representation of NEDs and executive directors, appropriate to the nature, scale and complexity of the business of the institution.
- In considering whether a risk committee is necessary, a company should assess factors such as: the needs of stakeholders, whether risk governance is aligned with strategy and the scope of the risk committee's responsibilities.
- If a company has both a risk and audit committee, there should be clear terms of reference separating the roles and responsibilities of both committees to ensure they both function effectively and do not overlap.

### 10 QUESTIONS TO HELP IMPROVE THE EFFECTIVENESS OF A RISK COMMITTEE

1. Do the models for risk adequately address low probability but high impact events?

2. Has the risk committee considered which scenario is the most challenging for the company?
3. Has the risk committee considered whether the board may need to amend the group strategic plan, including expectations of future growth and the group's ability to sustain or modify its business model?
4. Does the risk committee communicate regularly with the board and are these recommendations with regards to risk listened to and adhered to?
5. How does the board assess the independence of members and the chair of the committee?
6. Do board members have the required and specific experience necessary to sit on the risk committee?
7. Which risks will the committee oversee and which will be left to other committees?
8. Does the committee regularly keep abreast of regulatory changes that affect the company's risks?
9. Is the committee satisfied that the business presents the principal risks and uncertainties that most concern the board in a fair and transparent way?
10. Is risk a regular Board agenda item?

## Insights and Practical Suggestions: Risk Committees

In a high-risk business, such as a company manufacturing explosives or staff working in inclement conditions, this item should be the first on the agenda.

## The Corporate Governance Calendar

Regardless of the size of the company, it is good practice to set out in advance the yearly work programme for the board. This will help to determine how board time and committee time should be used given the legal calendar of events that every board must adhere to as well as the availability of board members.

Typically, most boards are overly ambitious in what can be achieved at each meeting, which is all the more reason for giving the work programme for the year due consideration.

The draft programme should be drawn up by the chairman, the chief executive and the Company Secretary and be presented to the board for discussion and approval at the start of the year.

The purpose of the sample calendar set out on the following page is to assist companies in developing the work programme.

## FIGURE 2: THE CORPORATE GOVERNANCE CALENDAR

(Assumes the financial year is the calendar.)

| | Jan | Feb | Mar | Apr | May | Jun | Jul | Aug | Sept | Oct | Nov | Dec |
|---|---|---|---|---|---|---|---|---|---|---|---|---|
| **AGM** | | | | | X | | | | | | | |
| **Board Meetings** | X | X | X | X | X | X | X | X | X | X | | X |
| **Management Team Meetings** | | X | | X | X | X | X | X | | X | X | X |
| **Remuneration Committee meetings** | | | X | | | | | | | | | |
| **Nomination Committee Meetings** | | X | | | | | | | X | | | |
| **Audit Committee Meetings** | X | | X | X | | | X | | | X | | |
| **Audit Committee Meetings with External Audit** | | | | | | | | | | X | | |
| **Risk Committee** | | | | | | X | | | X | | | |
| **Board and Management Team 'Away Day'** | | | | | | | | | | | X | |
| **Board 'Away Day'** | | | | | | | | X | | | | |
| **Board Evaluation** | | | | | | | | | X | | | |

95

# 5.

# Board Reporting

- The Importance of Good Information
- Categories of Information
- Practical Criteria for Board Papers
- Information for the Board
- Board Information Responsibilities
- Use of Board Time
- Presentation of Data
- 'Board Portals'

## The Importance of Good Information

Just about every code of governance refers to what the FRC describes as the need for the board to be "supplied in a timely manner with information in a form and of a quality appropriate to enable it to discharge its duties".[1]

It is imperative that the board are provided with information on the sector in which the organisation operates, the relative performance of the organisation within that sector as well as relevant aspects of its operations so that directors can get develop a deep understanding of the market to play a productive board role. Without real sectoral insight, the board's decisions will lack context and could be suboptimal.

The types of information that are required at board level typically include:

- strategic, e.g. market and competitor positioning;
- business performance information, i.e.:
  - financial
  - operational
  - sales and marketing
  - human resources
  - technology;
- external drivers of the business;
- key performance indicators;
- benchmarking information;
- risk information.

The balance of information presented to the board tends to focus on the management and operational rather than the strategic. Getting the balance right is critical to ensure that board decision-making is appropriate for the short, medium and longer terms.

## Categories of Information

The categories of information that need to be considered by the board are as set out below.

---

[1] *UK Corporate Governance Code* (FRC, 2014), para. B5.

## Information for Making Decisions

Issues brought to the board for decision should be supported by sufficient information for board members to make informed decisions. This process could take a number of meetings. Such decisions and related information could involve:

- market information for expansion overseas;
- financial information for investment in new plant or technology;
- capital markets information to raise new equity or capital.

## Information for Monitoring Performance

The board also needs to see how the organisation is doing against agreed key performance indicators (KPIs), examples of which are staff turnover at different levels, cash flow per employee, market share by product, percentage of business from new products, etc. This information should be in a form that makes it easy for board members to compare planned performance with actual performance. The 'balanced scorecard' (BSC) is one such tool that can be used. The BSC is a strategy performance management tool but tends to focus on KPIs in four key segments of the business, such as operations, staff, customers and finances. It is generally supported by automated tools to deliver the information. (Kaplan and Norton published a seminal book on the topic in 1996.[2])

## Information to Provide Environmental Context

This would involve contextual information allowing the board to have an understanding of the environment in which the organisation operates, the day-to-day work of the organisation and a greater insight into what key staff and units/divisions do.

## Practical Criteria for Board Papers

The following is a list of practical criteria for well-produced board papers[3]:

[2] Kaplan, Robert S., Norton, D.P., *The Balanced Scorecard, Translating Strategy into Action* (Boston, MA, Harvard Business School Press (1996)).

[3] See *Performance Reporting to Boards: A Guide to Good Practice* (CIMA, 2003).

## Clear, Concise and Digestible

Reports should be precise and succinct, in a form and of a quality appropriate to enable the board member to digest the information quickly, supported by the use of graphs and charts to enable them to discharge their duties effectively.

## Relevant

Information for inclusion should be pertinent to the matter, reflecting the organisation's principal objectives and strategy.

## Provide Perspective

Information should be presented within a relevant context. For example, market share of the company versus the competition and trends within relevant segments.

## Comparable

Reporting should include appropriate comparable data, e.g. prior-period contrasts, forecasts, performance against the competition, etc.

## Timely

Management should aim to deliver documentation for review to the board in a timely manner and provide any material information without delay. It is preferable for imperfect (but reasonably accurate) information to be received in good time, rather than flawless information too late.

## Reliable

Information should be comprehensive and unqualified so that the board can have confidence in it. The reliability of information will depend on its source, inclusiveness and integrity.

## Integrated

Integrated internal and external reporting demonstrates to the board the organisation's use of, and reliance on, different sources and relationships, and demonstrates the organisation's access to insightful information.

## Information for the Board

Typical information and documents provided to the board include:

- Agenda for the next meeting
- Minutes of the previous meeting (with a separate list of follow-up actions)
- The CEO's report
- The 'board pack' (see below for details of suggested contents)
- Board papers that require board input (for noting, discussion or decision).

### The CEO's Report

This will differ by company, depending on the nature of its activities, scale, geographic focus, etc.

Main headings and items typically included in the CEO's report are:

- Current Significant Issues
- Matters for Approval
- Strategic/Business Plan Update
- Key Performance Indicators
- Risk and Compliance Update
- Matters for Noting.

### The Board Pack

A board pack provides the members of a company with a clear and accurate perspective of the business's recent history and foreseeable future. The board pack must have the confidence of board members, in that what they read must be reliable and accurate, worthy of their time, their reflections, thoughts and discussions in preparing for board meetings.

The detailed contents of the board pack are typically as follows:

1. **Financial**   This section is typically prepared by the CFO in liaison with the chief executive.

The following information should be provided for each board meeting:

- income statement for the period under review and the year to date with results against budget and the prior year;
- balance sheet changes since last month and prior-year comparisons;
- cash flow statement for period under review and year to date;
- status of capital investments;
- update on funding strategy;
- analysis of key data against budgets;
- key performance indicators;
- projections and rolling forecast.

2. **Marketing, Sales and Operations**   This section will address all operational issues within the reporting period and is usually prepared by the head of operations. The key items to be addressed at a high level will be:

- key operational matters arising in the period under review;
- update on new initiatives to increase revenue and profile for the organisation;
- marketing and productivity information;
- status on key partnerships;
- update on significant challenges or opportunities facing the organisation.

3. **Human Resources**   This area will detail any employee issues, complaints, employee disputes, changes to structures, which have an impact on employees and any HR issues arising out of recent legislation.

4. **Risk Assurance**   The board should have a risk register, which should be revisited and 'kept alive' at each board meeting. This will highlight the key risks facing the organisation in terms of their probability of occurring and the impact on the organisation.

The risk register should highlight the following:

- key risks under respective headings (financial/operational/HR/ICT/reputational);
- key controls/policies in place to mitigate and manage these risks;
- rating of each risk according to agreed calibration;
- emerging risks;
- risks brought about by impending changes in political, environmental, technological, regulation, legislation, economic factors, etc.

103

5. **Governance** The FRC is responsible for the development of the *UK Corporate Governance Code* with which listed companies in Ireland and the UK must either comply or explain any non-compliance in their annual report. However, all organisations, whether listed or not, should report on their governance to their stakeholders against a code that is appropriate to them. For example, in Ireland all state-funded organisations must comply with the *Code of Practice for the Governance of State Bodies*.[4] Key areas of focus would be on remuneration and procurement.

This section of the board pack should address any governance matters that have arisen during the reporting period, such as:
- the extent to which the organisation complies with its relevant code, rules and policies;
- values, behaviour and conduct of the organisation;
- governance of the board and management;
- the manner in which the 'organisation does business';
- perceptions or otherwise of the organisation that may need to be addressed in the media or with the investment community.

6. **Information, Communication and Technology (ICT)** The board should receive a brief update from the Head of ICT on any matters arising in the period under review. The update may contain the following:
- details on the security and integrity of the ICT systems, data management and protection;
- details on the performance of the systems;
- issues arising from an ICT perspective;
- details of any proposed ICT investments;
- details of security steps, such as encryption of laptops, offsite back-ups, etc.;
- updates on website, portals, blogs, social media or any other online medium.

The contents of the board pack should be reviewed by the board on a regular basis to ensure that it is getting the information it needs in a form that is easily digestible.

---

[4] Department of Finance, October 2001; updated in June 2009.

# Board Information Responsibilities

As quoted from the FRC above, just about every code of governance refers to the need for the board to be "supplied in a timely manner with information in a form and of a quality appropriate to enable it to discharge its duties".

When the FRC drafted the latest version of the *UK Corporate Governance Code* it introduced some significant changes in relation to the provision of information. Some commentators speculated that this change was precipitated by non-executive directors who defended their performance during the recent economic crisis by claiming that management presented incomplete (or, in some cases, misleading) information to the board and they could not have acted any differently from the way they did.

In summary, responsibilities in relation to information flows to the board include the following:

- **The chairman** is now charged with "responsibility for ensuring that the directors receive accurate, timely and clear information".[5]
- **The Company Secretary** "Under the direction of the chairman, the Company Secretary's responsibilities include ensuring good information flows within the board and its committees and between senior management and non-executive directors, as well as facilitating induction and assisting with professional development as required."[6]
- **The CFO** has a particular responsibility to deliver high quality information to the board on the financial position of the company.
- **Non-executive directors** should insist on receiving high quality information sufficiently in advance so that there can be thorough consideration of the issues prior to, and informed debate and challenge at, board meetings. High quality information is that which is appropriate for making decisions on the issue at hand – it should be accurate, clear, comprehensive, up-to-date and timely. It should contain a summary of the contents of any paper, and inform the director of what is expected of him or her on that issue.

---

[5] *UK Corporate Governance Code* (FRC, 2014), para. B5.
[6] *Ibid.*

## Use of Board Time

While this is not an exact science, in my experience over the course of a year a board should allocate time broadly as follows:

- Company administration: 15%
- Strategy: 40%
- Business performance: 30%
- Any other business 15%.

Some organisations allow time at board meetings every now and again for members to bring up matters that are not on the agenda but are relevant to the future success of the organisation.

## Presentation of Data

Most board packs tend to be paper-based, with a focus on the financials. To assist in the presentation of a broader spectrum of data, organisations should consider using a 'dashboard', which, according to Stephen Few in his book *Information Dashboard Design*[7]:

> "… is a visual display of the most important information needed to achieve one or more objectives and arranged on a single screen so the information can be monitored at a glance."

An effective dashboard enables users to understand current matters, tasks and projects at a glance, based on the most important and relevant metrics, such as product margins, account performances, management costs and other critical information that affects or is needed to achieve business objectives, such as improving return on investment, customer service levels, cash flow, etc.

There are many providers of dashboard tools in the market. They can be used to improve the effectiveness of board meetings because the information presented is based on key metrics that are aligned with the strategic and annual business plans.

---

[7] Few, S., *Information Dashboard Design: The Effective Visual Communication of Data* (O'Reilly Media, January 2006).

## 'Board Portals'

A 'board portal' is a web-based, online workspace devoted exclusively to the board. Directors can access confidential board materials on the portal at any time and from any location. Security controls keep board documents and members' communications protected and confidential.

The main benefit of using a portal is the reduction in time and cost of producing and managing board materials.

Some organisations develop their own custom-made programs while others choose to buy a board portal from outside vendors. Typical features offered by board portals include document access and management, calendar management and meeting scheduling, alerts, survey tools, note-taking, version control, online discussion and virtual meeting capability.

# 6.
# Risk Management

- **Background**
- **Definition**
- **Risk Appetite**
- **Risk Appetite Statements, Company Objectives and Risk Maturity**
- **What are the Categories of Risk that need to be Managed?**
- **Risk Management Techniques**
- **Role of the Board in Managing Risk**
- **Risk Committees**
- **Monitoring Exposure to Risks**

## Background

Lessons learned following the global financial crisis include the importance of establishing an effective risk oversight at the board level.[1]

The big and basic risk governance question is:

* Do we express clearly and comprehensively the extent of our willingness to take risk in order to meet our strategic and business objectives?

## Definition

'Risk' in this context is defined as the probability of encountering an event that might adversely affect the achievement of the organisation's objectives. In very basic terms, a risk is some jeopardy or threat, about which there is some ambiguity, which can stop one from getting from point A to point B.

As companies are set up to achieve superior returns, with limited liability to risk takers, it follows that the currency of corporate governance is in setting objectives, superior strategy execution, risk management and reward. The challenge for the board is to assess the degree of risk it is willing to take to achieve the strategic objectives and the rewards sought on behalf of the shareholders.

There are many types of objective, for example financial, customer service, product innovation, market penetration, safety, etc. There are multiple risks (strategic, financial, operational, hazard, etc.) to each type of objective. There are, however, only two types of uncertainty or ambiguity:

* measurable uncertainties; and
* unmeasurable uncertainties

### *Measurable Uncertainties*

These are inherently insurable in the insurance market because they occur independently (e.g. traffic accidents, house fires, theft, etc.) and with sufficient frequency as to be reckonable using traditional

---

[1] Risk Management International.

statistical methods sufficient to reasonably and confidently project likelihood and consequence.

Measurable uncertainties are treated individually through risk management, which assesses the potential final outcome and losses, which may be mitigated through insurance.

Measurable uncertainties are ultimately funded out of insurance premiums, which are charged to the profit and loss account.

## Unmeasurable Uncertainties

Unmeasurable uncertainties are inherently *un*-insurable using traditional methods because they are often people-based and networked in nature (i.e. cause A precipitates cause B) and occur with irregular frequency (e.g. supply chain/critical service provider interruption, etc.).

Unmeasurable uncertainties are treated on a broad basis through organisational resilience. For the top five to 15 corporate risks that are typically inestimable in terms of likelihood of occurrence, the organisation seeks to maintain an ability to absorb and respond to shocks and surprises, and to deliver credible solutions before reputation is damaged and stakeholders lose confidence.

Unmeasurable uncertainties or risks are those that ultimately have a negative effect on the balance sheet.

It is the unanticipated consequences of unidentified risks that will challenge the common sense and experience of the board and the executive management team. Risk management is the process whereby the company minimises the chances of that event happening.

Today's hyper-connected and multispeed world is driving the effect of unmeasurable uncertainties on company objectives to new, unprecedented heights. For example, few boards really understand the impact or potential of digital media. Consequently, they struggle to assess the risks associated with it or the speed at which risk can spread globally. A mobile-phone video of inappropriate senior executive behaviour can create havoc if it goes viral and can lead to reputational damage within minutes.

Clearly, there are more unmeasurable uncertainties affecting objectives than measurable uncertainties.

There are three principle organisational responses to assessing and managing risk:

1. clearer definition of mission critical objectives that must be protected, at all costs;
2. threat and risk mapping, providing earlier identification and reporting of threats and risks; and
3. realistic proving and testing of management's capability to deliver credible solutions should events occur.

## Risk Appetite

Risk appetite is defined as "the amount and type of risk that an organisation is willing to pursue or retain".[2]

Risk tolerance is the "organisation's readiness to bear the risk in order to achieve its objectives".[3]

Clearly, the terms 'risk appetite' and 'risk tolerance' are interrelated. The relationship between the two terms is as follows:

• the universe of risks for a company is particular to its strategic direction;
• within the universe of risks lies a narrow band of limits (tolerances) either side (upside and downside) of the strategic direction set by the company;
• risk appetite is a much narrower band of limits (*within* risk tolerance) which the company is willing to pursue or retain in pursuit of its strategic direction.

Threats to both the business model and reputation increase significantly when a company strays outside of its stated risk appetite.

Lessons learned from and in the aftermath of the 2008 global financial crisis include recognising the potential consequences to a company, its stakeholders, directors and officers should the board of directors fail to articulate, and adhere to, its risk appetite in the form of risk appetite statements for principal mission critical objectives.

---

[2] ISO Guide 73 2009(en) – Risk Management Vocabulary Section 3.7.1.2.
[3] *Ibid.* Section 3.7.1.3.

## Risk Appetite Statements, Company Objectives and Risk Maturity

Risk appetite statements are difficult to design and articulate, and are sensitive to changes in the business environment. Ordinarily, they will only emerge as living, practical guides to company decision-making when developed collaboratively between the corporate entity and its subsidiaries or business units, and thereafter monitored by the board risk committee. Risk appetite statements should not be developed by an element of a business in isolation.

Board risk appetite statements are high level in nature and express the "nature and extent of the significant risks [the board] is willing to take in achieving strategic objectives".[4]

Business-unit and sub-unit risk appetite statements tend more to reflect how subsidiary mission statements are executed within pre-ordained tolerances set at the corporate level.

Clearly, before risk appetite statements can be developed, understood and agreed, 'company objectives' must first be expressly stated and agreed.

The process whereby company objectives are expressly stated and agreed requires that strong leadership, integrity and challenge are exercised before the risk management process can truly commence. In this regard, it should be understood that risk management and corporate governance are reverse sides of the same coin and closely related.

In essence, without effective risk management, corporate governance has no teeth. This understanding of the relationship between corporate governance and risk management is becoming more demonstrably evident with the evolution of corporate governance codes around the world (post the 2008 crisis). This is particularly so in the UK and Ireland, where, arguably, the FRC is poised to establish a new global benchmark in corporate governance following its release in November 2013 of a new consultation on draft guidance

---

[4] ISO Guide 73 2009(en) – Risk Management Vocabulary.

to directors of companies applying the *UK Corporate Governance Code* and associated changes to the Code.[5]

In summary, there are five tests that directors should apply in reviewing their organisation's risk appetite statement.[6]

## FIVE TESTS FOR RISK APPETITE STATEMENTS

1. Do the managers making decisions understand the degree to which they (individually) are permitted to expose the organisation to the consequences of an event or situation? Any risk appetite statement needs to be practical, guiding managers to make risk-intelligent decisions.
2. Do the executives understand their aggregated and inter-linked level of risk so they can determine whether it is acceptable or not?
3. Do the board and executive leadership understand the aggregated and interlinked level of risk for the organisation as a whole?
4. Are both managers and executives clear that risk appetite is not constant? It changes as the environment and business conditions change. Anything approved by the board must have some flexibility built in.
5. Are risk decisions made with full consideration of reward? The risk appetite framework needs to help managers and executives take an appropriate level of risk for the business, given the potential for reward.

It is the unanticipated consequences of unidentified risks that challenge the common sense and experience of the board and the executive management team. Risk management is the process whereby the company minimises the chances of that event happening.

---

[5] *Risk Management, Internal Control and the Going Concern Basis of Accounting* (FRC, Consultation Paper, November 2013).

[6] Institute of Risk Management, *Risk Appetite and Tolerance* (guidance paper, September 2011).

## What are the Categories of Risk that need to be Managed?

Risks can arise in many forms. They can include the following:

- Financial – cash loss, credit risk exposure, interest rate exposure, credit availability, etc.
- Human – over-reliance on key members of staff, self-interest of directors/employees, etc.
- Operational – e.g. the breakdown of a key business process.
- Technological – breakdown of firewalls, data integrity, etc.
- Physical – fire, hazardous waste, unsafe buildings, etc.
- Intangible – reputation and brand, etc.

This list by no means covers all the risks to which a company is exposed. Its purpose is to highlight that there are different *categories* of risk. Each company will be exposed to a different set of risks. How it decides to manage these risks will depend on the attitude to risk by the board and the executive management team. Needless to say, the risks a business is exposed to can change depending on its market position, the economic environment and its own financial strength.

## Risk Management Techniques

Common risk management techniques include the following:

- **Avoid** – redesign the process to avoid particular risks with the objective of reducing overall risk.
- **Diversify** – Spread the risk among numerous assets or processes to reduce the overall risk of loss or impairment.
- **Control** – Design activities to prevent, detect or contain adverse events or to promote positive outcomes.
- **Share** – Distribute a portion of the risk through a contract with another party, such as insurance.
- **Transfer** – Distribute all of the risk through a contract with another party, such as outsourcing.
- **Accept** – Allow minor risks to exist and thus avoid spending more on managing the risks than on the potential harm.

## Role of the Board in Managing Risk

A key fiduciary duty of the board is to protect shareholder assets and guide the company in achieving its objectives:

> "The board is responsible for determining the nature and extent of the significant risks it is willing to take in achieving its strategic objectives."[7]

The key steps in managing risk for the board and the executive management team are as follows:

- Develop a risk appetite statement
- Identify the risks
- Develop a risk management policy
- Develop a risk management strategy
- Implement the strategy
- Monitor the risks
- Develop a contingency plan
- Ensure that there is a crisis management system in place.

Depending on the size of the company, risk management may be the responsibility of a member of the executive management team, a board member, the audit committee or the company may have its own risk committee.

## Risk Committees

Revised corporate governance codes and best practice now mean that all financial institutions are required to establish a risk committee, separate to the standard audit committee.

While this is not a regulatory requirement for other organisations in different industries, it is nonetheless crucial that an appropriate regulatory or oversight body addresses these issues. Every organisation should assess its own individual circumstances before considering a risk committee.

(We have explored the roles and requirements of risk committees in **Chapter 4,** Building Blocks of Corporate Governance.)

---

[7] *UK Corporate Governance Code* (FRC, 2014).

## Monitoring Exposure to Risks

In order to safeguard against significant risks, every organisation should introduce a 'trigger point', beyond which a particular strategy is reviewed and/or abandoned. The risk appetite statement will form the context for these trigger points. Organisations should also conduct 'what if' scenarios to test risk assumptions.

Organisations should also put in place assurance frameworks that assess the controls in place to minimise risk. This provides proof that the control in place is working effectively. This evaluation could be a report from management, audit/risk committees or the external auditor and will outline any gaps in the risk management plan.

### 10 QUESTIONS THAT RISK MANAGEMENT SHOULD ADDRESS

1. What is the biggest risk the company is exposed to today?
2. If that risk were to occur, what are the implications for the business?
3. Who is responsible for risk management and what experience does that person have?
4. When was the last time the risk management plan was updated?
5. How often is risk monitored at board level?
6. Is the focus of our risk management on mission-critical risks or are we trying to cover too many?
7. What was the last major risk the business was exposed to and what can we learn from how we managed it?
8. Can we learn from the experience of risks our competitors have been exposed to, and perhaps did not manage well?
9. Do we have an early warning system on the mission-critical risks?
10. Do we have a 'trigger point' approach to risk?

# 7.

# Evaluating Board Performance

- **Why Evaluate the Board?**
- **What Should be Evaluated?**
- **How can the Board be Evaluated?**
- **Practical Suggestions**
- **Getting Started**

## Why Evaluate the Board?

Boards should undertake formal and rigorous evaluations of their performance and that of individual directors. These evaluations are of enormous benefit as they can improve a board's performance and accountability.

For example, a board's performance can be measured in a number of ways, including:

- performance against the strategic plan and key milestones;
- key financial metrics;
- increase in shareholder value;
- achievement of progress against the board's annual work plan;
- improvements in customer/stakeholder feedback/satisfaction, etc.

Given the effort and cost that goes into preparing for and holding each board meeting, it is important to look back on a regular basis to assess how well the board has performed and to what extent it has added value to the company/organisation.

Boards should conduct a formal evaluation of their performance annually. This can be conducted in a number of ways, which will be outlined below. Irish banks and credit institutions are required under the Central Bank's corporate governance code to formally review their overall performance and that of their individual directors annually. An external evaluation of their performance is required every three years to ensure that the review is objective and independent.

Apart from being a clear demonstration of good governance, the reasons for evaluating board performance are as follows:

- assessing the organisation's corporate governance framework;
- assessing the relevance of the current skills, knowledge, experience, and the composition of the board;
- addressing specific governance issues affecting the organisation;
- identifying any weaknesses that can be remedied by board training and development;
- assessing the adequacy of the information flowing to the board or being disseminated to shareholders and stakeholders;
- assessing if the board is performing to the best of its ability;

- challenging over-dominant directors;
- benchmarking performance against other peer organisations;
- assessing if the board has delivered upon the strategic objectives of the organisation;
- assessing the board's decision-making process.

## THE EVALUATION PROCESS: KEY ISSUES TO ADDRESS BEFORE STARTING

- Who will conduct the evaluation, and is he or she independent?
- What will the process be?
- What is the timescale?
- What methodologies will be used?
- How will the results be processed?
- How will confidentiality be safeguarded?

## What Should be Evaluated?

The following should be evaluated and assessed:

- performance of the board as a collective unit;
- individual performance of each member of the board, including the chairman;
- performance and effectiveness of board committees;
- achievement of the strategy of the company;
- extent to which the board has the appropriate risk management framework in place and the supporting internal controls;
- board communication with shareholders and stakeholders;
- composition of the board and future requirements;
- boardroom processes and procedures, e.g the decision-making process;
- the principles and values of the company (see **Chapter 3**);
- the quality of information provided to the board and its committees (see **Chapter 5**);
- key board relationships, i.e. between the chairman, committee chairs, the chief executive and the executive management team.

## How can the Board be Evaluated?

The chairman is responsible for ensuring that a board evaluation is conducted on a regular basis. He or she should choose an appropriate approach and act on its outcomes.

There are a number of very practical ways in which the board can be evaluated. These could include one or a combination of the following:

- **Self-assessment**  This is likely to be of limited benefit, but will raise the awareness levels of the board members on issues that affect performance.
- **Questionnaires**  These could be developed, analysed and summarised by the chairman, Company Secretary or an agreed non-executive director. As well as direct relevance of the questions, the main concern here is to ensure the confidentiality of the responses. The nominated board member feeds back the summarised results from the questionnaire to the board for discussion and action, if required.
- **360 Degree Feedback**  The board members assess the performance of the board and also that of their colleagues using a form of questionnaire.
- **Interviews with Board Members**  These could be conducted by the chairman, Company Secretary or an agreed non-executive director. Board members should be interviewed individually and confidentially and the key issues can then be fed back to the board for discussion.
- **Boardroom Discussion**  This can be led by the chairman or an independent facilitator.
- **Benchmarking**  The purpose of benchmarking is to assess how the performance of the board compares against best practice and comparable organisations. (Of course, work should be carried out beforehand on defining carefully what it is being benchmarked against.)
- **External Evaluation**  This is perhaps the most rigorous method as an external evaluator, experienced in assessing the performance of boards, can bring greater independence and objectivity.

## Practical Suggestions

The key issues arising in the review of board performance will need to be considered very carefully, with particular attention paid to how the information will be communicated to the board and its members. The chairman will have a critical role in this, particularly in relation to the more sensitive issues.

Any review of the board should be approached in a positive frame of mind to ensure that the review is conducted in the right spirit.

The process should have clear objectives, be well planned and confidential. The board should be provided with information as to what will be reviewed, who will conduct the evaluation, the nature of the process and how key findings will be communicated to the board and then addressed. PLCs are required under the *UK Corporate Governance Code* to disclose in the annual report how the performance evaluation of the board and its committees has been conducted. If an external facilitator was used, his or her identity and a statement as to whether he or she has any connection with the company are also required.

The evaluation process should be tailored to meet the specific needs of the organisation. All findings and lessons from the evaluation should be followed up and enacted.

## Getting Started

Clearly, before commencing any review work, there should be consensus on the need for and the benefits of evaluation. The next step is to select a leader to champion a process with which everyone is comfortable.

If the evaluation is being done for the first time, it may make sense to seek input from all the board directors and leading members of the executive management team on what to evaluate and how to evaluate it. It might also be worth finding out what other organisations do, so as not to 'reinvent the wheel'. There may well be non-executive directors with experience on other boards whose expertise can be utilised.

Whichever is chosen, it is the process or method that is to be used to evaluate the board that should be disclosed publicly rather than the outcomes, which should only be discussed amongst board members themselves.

## 10 QUESTIONS THAT AN EVALUATION OF THE BOARD SHOULD ADDRESS

1. How well is the board performing?
2. Does the board have the appropriate skills and experience to support strategy of the company?
3. Does the company have the right committees in place?
4. Is the board getting the right information to assess company performance?
5. If the company were to appoint a new board, how many members of this board would it reappoint?
6. Is there a succession plan?
7. Does the board spend enough time on the critical strategic issues?
8. Does the board add real value to the company?
9. What are the views of the main stakeholders on the performance of the board?
10. Will the evaluation process lead to actions?

# 8.

# Priorities for Improving Corporate Governance

- Introduction
- Leadership from the Top on Ethics and Values
- Governance Structures that are Fit for Purpose
- Greater Professionalisation of the Board
- A Real Focus on Improving Measurable Board Performance
- A Step Change in the Quality of Information presented to the Board
- Increase Diversity to Improve Quality of Board Debate and Decision-making
- Get Real about Risk

## Introduction

Corporate governance practices have changed dramatically in the years since the *Cadbury Report* in 1992. Financial crises, increased regulatory burdens, corporate failures and public intolerance of poor standards in high places mean that the expectations of shareholders and stakeholders of all types of organisations that have a board or oversight body are higher than ever.

Given Ireland's ambition to be the best small country in the world in which to do business and our reliance on foreign direct investment, it is critical that the country is seen as a leader in the development and enforcement of corporate governance standards.

This chapter highlights seven priorities for organisations with a real ambition to improve their corporate governance:

1. Leadership from the top on ethics and values.
2. Governance structures that are fit for purpose.
3. Greater professionalisation of the board.
4. A real focus on improving measurable board performance.
5. A step change in the quality and presentation of information to the board.
6. Improving the quality of board debate and decision-making through increased diversity.
7. Getting real about risk.

## 1. Leadership from the Top on Ethics and Values

The direction, strategy and integrity of any organisation are dictated by its leadership. In recent years, scandals involving chairmen and chief executives have highlighted the need to pay more attention to the ethics and core values of organisations.

We would like to see:

• Increased emphasis on the formal adoption of ethics and values that are embedded in the 'DNA' of the organisation.

The chairman of the board plays the decisive role in establishing or shaping the future ethics and values of the organisation. For this to be real, sustainable and capable of implementation, the

129

organisation must go through a process to document its ethics and values in a manner that makes it easy for those ethics and values to be lived and made operational. Staff at all levels must live and breathe values and be accountable for them.

An organisation with sound ethics and strong core values will generally be a more sustainable one, as staff and potential staff members are likely to be more comfortable working with others who share the same values.

- The board 'walking the talk' when it comes to ethics.

At every opportunity, all directors should be encouraged to communicate the company's ethics and values and the importance of their application to the company, both internally and externally.

Communication is not just about words: 'walking the talk' is also important. It means applying the code of ethics to directors' behaviour, as well as to staff conduct. How does the board handle conflicts of interests? Is there transparency over board appointments? Is remuneration and recruitment fair and transparent?

## 2. Governance Structures that are Fit for Purpose

Organisations should 'stand back' and ask: if we were to start the organisation again, would we have the same structures and board composition that we have today? In other words, are our current governance structures fit for purpose?

Key questions to be addressed would include:

- How many of the current board would transfer to a new board?
- What would be the new board rotation policy?
- What size does the board really need to be?
- How many executive directors should be on it, if any?
- How many committees do we really need?

This review should be carried out on a regular basis, ideally by experienced external board evaluation professionals who have no vested interest in the outcome.

## 3. Greater Professionalisation of the Board

In Ireland, we still have some distance to travel to a point where we truly value and respect good corporate governance that is based on deep-rooted and closely held values. While we have some great examples of corporate governance on a world stage in organisations such as CRH, the IDA and others, we have a lot to learn, whether it be in the State, non-profit or private sectors.

The governance models that are appropriate to organisations in these sectors will be different, but at the same time they will have a number of common characteristics. To improve the practice and effectiveness of corporate governance, a number of small but important changes are required, as set out below.

### Smaller Boards

Too many publicly funded and non-profit organisations in Ireland have boards with up to, and in some cases exceeding, 35 members. The numbers of board members in such organisations are driven up by the need to accommodate representative or factional interests either on an elected or appointed basis. In many instances, the individuals have great difficulty in recognising that they are collegiate members of a board with all the obligations that that entails, rather than being there to represent the constituency from whence they came and its interests.

In our opinion, boards with more than 12 directors are likely to be too large for effective decision-making. In boards with more than 12 members, members cease to take personal responsibility for the group's actions and rely on others to take the lead, particularly where some individuals have a specialist skill or particularly relevant experience. Large groups also inhibit consensus building, which is the way the best boards should operate. The more members there are, the harder it is to reach agreement, and so fewer decisive actions are taken, which could be critical in responding to market or environmental challenges.

Research on group dynamics suggests that smaller groups are the most effective at decision-making. They are small enough for all members to take personal responsibility for the group's actions and they can usually reach a consensus in a reasonably short time. These advantages of small size outweigh the potential benefits of having extra generalists on a large board.

Ideally, the number of members on any board should be between eight to 12 members. The exact number should be driven by the nature of the organisation, board workload, number of committees to be supported and the capability of the executive.

## A Majority of the Board should be Independent Non-executive Directors

There is a strong argument for greater separation of the duties and roles of the board and the executive. Many boards have a number of the executive directors on them, some for no apparent governance reason. For some organisations, however, it is a way of rewarding loyalty, recognising performance or retaining key management talent.

For corporate governance to work well, it is important that the lines between the role of the board and the role of the executive are as clearly drawn as possible. Ideally, the board would be composed solely of independent directors, with the executive management team represented by the chief executive. Other members of the executive could attend when necessary.

Having a higher proportion of NEDs than executive directors ensures that the board focuses more on overall strategy and on the 'bigger picture' rather than management or operational detail, unless when absolutely necessary.

## Public Sector Director Appointments based on Talent rather than Representation or Political Interests

Publicly funded boards in Ireland have been criticised for making politically motivated appointments without due process being followed. While the quality of appointments to State boards is improving, it needs to go further.

Directors should always be appointed on merit and capability and never with political motivation in mind or the need to satisfy representative interests. To ensure greater transparency in the appointment of directors to State boards, it is important that a process is put in place that facilitates this.

## 4. A Real Focus on Improving Measurable Board Performance

The effort and cost in running the board of an organisation is generally underestimated. Consequently, any productivity gain should have a direct impact on the performance of the organisation.

In order to maximise their potential and productivity, boards need to constantly work on improving their performance and efficiency. This performance can be assessed by conducting an internal evaluation annually with an in-depth, externally commissioned process every three years (see **Chapter 7**).

There are a number of dimensions in which board performance can be enhanced, including:

- enhancing the quality of the chair and the 'chairing';
- continuously improving board capability through regular board renewal;
- ensuring that the talent in the boardroom is put to best use;
- improving board and committee productivity with:
  - annual work plans,
  - agenda and minutes,
  - appropriate information flows;
- development of supporting management tools, such as:
  - a strategic plan,
  - an implementation plan,
  - annual business plans,
  - a risk register;
- measuring the board's performance in a number of ways, including:
  - performance against the strategic plan and key implementation milestones,
  - key financial metrics,
  - relative increase in shareholder value,
  - achievement of progress against the board's annual work plan,
  - improvements in customer/stakeholder feedback/satisfaction etc.

## 5. A Step Change in the Quality of Information presented to the Board

Boards face critical challenges in ensuring that they actually receive accurate information about the performance of their organisation. In order to improve the flow of information, we recommend the following:

### *An Annual Review of the Board Pack*

Board packs (see **Chapter 6**) and reports are often too 'figure heavy', are filled with information about backdated financials and briefing memos which often reach hundreds of pages in extent.

In order to make this information clearer and more relevant, boards should consider carrying out an annual review of their information requirements, how it should be presented and structured to help board productivity.

In reporting, *quality* is definitely preferable to quantity. A study in the UK found that the average board report for PLCs was 288 pages long and would take nine hours to read.[1] While much of this information may be important, boards need to be able to digest reports quickly before meetings.

### *Proactive Use of Modern Technology*

There is an abundance of devices and software that can help improve the flow and presentation of information, such as the 'dashboards' mentioned earlier in **Chapter 5**.

Many boards now receive their board pack on iPads or other tablets, or through online 'board portals'. These mechanisms provide a great opportunity to use graphics to make data easy to assimilate and comprehend. It also means information can be sent to board members anywhere in the country or the world, quickly and easily.

Furthermore, annual reports should be made available across a variety of mediums, online through PDF download, on a specific organisation 'app', as well as in more traditional forms.

---

[1] See http://video.ft.com/2346686287001/Non-executives-need-tools-for-job/companies

## 6. Increase Diversity to Improve Quality of Board Debate and Decision-making

When a board becomes overly homogenous, there is a real danger that its effectiveness will be greatly reduced as the breadth and depth of thinking and insight that is required to make it successful could be compromised. Diversity can only enhance this. We recommend the following:

### *A Variety of Industry and Functional Backgrounds*

Boards should be comprised of individuals with a range of differing backgrounds from different industries, disciplines and functions that will directly support the strategy of the business.

### *Variety of Nationalities*

Boards should appoint non-nationals in order to give increased outsider perspectives for Irish organisations that operate abroad, bringing a local and cultural insight that may prove vital in new markets.

If an organisation is considering expanding its operation to a certain country, its board should seek to appoint directors from that country. For example, if an Irish NGO wanted to work in Nigeria, it should think of appointing a Nigerian NED to advise on moving into this new territory.

### *Gender Diversity*

There remains a gender imbalance on many boards in Ireland, where men vastly outnumber women; 70% of women say it is more difficult for a woman to become a NED in Ireland.[2] A board should at least be more reflective of the gender balance of their organisation's employees, customer base, etc. If it is not, greater efforts need to be made by the organisation to address this issue. In fact, the EU has

---

[2] *Women on Boards in Ireland: Insights from women directors on the progress made and obstacles remaining* (Institute of Directors in Ireland, January 2013).

outlined board gender targets of at least 40% women. While quotas alone are not the answer to the issue, the threat of them may be!

## Variety in Skill Sets

Boards should ensure that they have a range of directors who have specific skills in different areas. This means there should be some directors with relevant experience in financial management, innovation, raising capital, risk management, strategy implementation, audit, etc.

## An 'Outlier'

Boards may also want to consider appointing an individual who may not fit any of the above criteria, but who can bring some intellectual 'horsepower' to the board to assist the colour of the debate. For example, recruiting a NED with an ability and intellect to think deeply about topics about which he or she may have no first-hand experience but to which he or she can nevertheless bring new perspectives.

## 7. Get Real about Risk

As discussed in **Chapter 6**, risk management is relevant to all organisations, not just the larger ones.

The world is ever changing: cybercrime, the expanding digital footprint, global warming, the importance of brand, greater global financial systemic risk – all make for an environment that is more uncertain.

Successful businesses are resilient businesses that can identify and manage risk.

The job of the board is to ensure that risk is kept alive on the agenda in a manner that gets the attention of the organisation. The attention span of board members for risk registers and the detail beneath them can be limited, so securing their engagement is vital. This should be done in a manner that is real world and not perceived as an academic or box-ticking exercise.

# Appendices

A1 – Key Points from Corporate Governance Codes and Reports

A2 – Corporate Governance Checklists

A3 – Matters Reserved for the Board

A4 – Sample Terms of Reference for Board Committees and the Executive Management Committee

- Audit Committee: Sample Terms of Reference
- Nomination Committee: Sample Terms of Reference
- Remuneration Committee: Sample Terms of Reference
- Risk Committee: Sample Terms of Reference
- Sample Charter for an Executive Management Committee

A5 – Sample Letter of Non-executive Director Appointment

A6 – Sample Outline for an Organisation's Code of Ethics

A7 – Case Studies

- The Abbey Theatre
- FÁS
- Irish Nationwide Building Society
- Neath vs Ospreys
- Tallaght Hospital

# A1.

# Key Points from Corporate Governance Codes and Reports

- The Cadbury Report

- The Greenbury Report

- The Hampel Committee Report

- The Turnbull Report

- The Combined Code

- The Higgs Report

- Smith Report

- The Combined Code

- Walker Review (2009)

- The UK Corporate Governance Code 2010

- The UK Stewardship Code 2010

- Irish Corporate Governance Annex

- Governance Code for Credit Institutions and Insurance Undertakings

- Companies Bill 2012

- Charities Act 2009

- EU Green Paper – The EU Corporate Governance Framework

- The UK Corporate Governance Code 2014

# The Cadbury Report (December 1992)[1]

## *Key Areas of Focus*

- Financial aspects of corporate governance
- Control and reporting functions of the board
- Role of the auditors

## *Key Recommendations*

- The board should meet regularly and retain full and effective control over the company and monitor its executive management team.
- There should be clear divisions of responsibility so that no one individual has unfettered powers of decision.
- The board should include non-executive directors (NEDs) of sufficient calibre and number for their views to carry sufficient weight in the board's decisions.
- The board should have a formal schedule of matters specifically reserved to it for decisions.
- Directors should be able to take independent professional advice at the company's expense. They should also have access to the advice and services of the Company Secretary.
- NEDs should bring an independent judgement to bear on issues of strategy, performance, resources (including key appointments) and standards of conduct.
- The majority of directors should be independent of the executive management team and free from any business or other relationship.
- NEDs should be nominated for fixed terms and reappointment should not be automatic.
- NEDs should be selected through a formal process and their appointment should be a matter for the board as a whole.
- Directors' service contracts should not exceed three years without shareholder approval.
- Director's total emoluments and those of the chairman, including pension contributions and share options, should

---

[1] *Report of the Committee on the Financial Aspects of Corporate Governance* ('The Cadbury Report' (Gee Publishing, 1992)).

be disclosed. Separate figures should be given for salary and performance-related elements and the basis on which performance is measured should be explained.

- Executive directors' pay should be subject to the recommendations of a remuneration committee made up wholly or mainly of NEDs.
- The board should establish an audit committee of at least three NEDs, with written terms of reference.
- The directors should explain their responsibility for preparing the accounts next to a statement by the auditors about their reporting responsibilities.
- Interim reports should include balance sheet information and should be reviewed by the auditors.
- Fees paid to auditors for non-audit work should be disclosed.
- The accountancy profession should draw up guidelines on the rotation of auditors.
- The directors should report on the effectiveness of the company's system of internal control.
- Directors should state in the report and accounts that the business is a going concern and the assumptions on which this statement is based.
- The UK Government should introduce legislation protecting auditors who report reasonable suspicion of fraud to the regulatory authorities.

## The Greenbury Report (July 1995)[2]

### *Key Area of Focus*

- Directors' remuneration

### *Key Recommendations*

- Executive pay should be set by a remuneration committee made up solely of NEDs with no personal financial interest (other than as shareholders) in the matters to be decided.

---

[2] *Directors' Remuneration: Report of a Study Group Chaired by Sir Richard Greenbury* (Gee Publishing, 1995).

- Membership of the remuneration committee should be listed each year in the committee's report to shareholders.
- The remuneration committee should report to shareholders each year in the annual report.
- The annual report should include full details of each director's pay package, including basic salary, benefits-in-kind, pension entitlements, annual bonuses, share options, etc.
- Any service contracts in excess of one year should be disclosed and the reasons for the longer notice periods explained.
- All long-term incentive plans, including share options, should be approved by shareholders.
- Performance-related pay should be designed to align the interests of directors with those of shareholders and to give directors the incentive to perform at the highest level.
- Share options should be phased rather than awarded in one large block.
- Executive share options should never be issued at a discount.
- Bonuses and benefits-in-kind should not be pensionable.
- Notice and contract periods should be reduced to one year or less. However, remuneration committees should be flexible – in some cases, notice or contract periods of up to two years may be acceptable.

## The Hampel Committee Report (January 1998)[3]

### Key Areas of Focus

- The role of directors
- Directors' remuneration
- Shareholders and the AGM
- Accountability and audit.

### Key Recommendations

- The majority of non-executive directors (NEDs) should be independent and the annual report should specify which directors are considered to be independent.

---

[3] *Committee on Corporate Governance – Final Report* (Gee Publishing, 1998).

- NEDs should make up at least one-third of the membership of the board.
- Boards should introduce procedures to monitor their own performance and that of individual directors.
- NEDs should come from a wide range of backgrounds.
- The roles of chairman and chief executive should ideally be separated. Where the two roles are combined, the company should justify its decision.
- A senior NED should be identified in the annual report to whom shareholder concerns, which are not being addressed by the chairman, can be conveyed.
- All directors should submit themselves to re-election at least every three years.
- There should be no fixed rules for length of service or age of NEDs.
- New directors should be recommended to the board by a nomination committee.
- Each company should have an audit committee consisting of at least three NEDs, of whom at least two are independent.
- Audit firms should not have more than 10% of their income coming from any one public interest client.

## The Turnbull Report (September 1999)[4]

### Key Areas of Focus

- Guidance for directors on the *Combined Code*
- Internal control
- Risk management.

### Key Recommendations

- The board is responsible for internal control and ensuring that the system is effective in managing risk.
- Internal control should be embedded in the company and not be treated as a separate exercise.

---

[4] *Internal Control: Guidance for Directors on the Combined Code* (ICAEW, 1999; FRC, revised 2005).

- Internal control effectiveness should be monitored and subject to regular review by the board.
- Companies that do not have an internal audit function should review the need for one on an annual basis.
- Companies should identify, evaluate and manage their significant risks.
- The management team are responsible for managing risks through maintaining an effective system of internal control and the board as a whole is responsible for reporting on it.

## The Combined Code (June 1998)[5]

The *Combined Code of Corporate Governance* (1998) combined, replaced and refined the earlier recommendations of the Cadbury, Greenbury and Hampel Committees on corporate governance.

### *Key Areas of Focus*

- Directors
- The board
- The chairman and chief executive
- Board balance
- Supply of information
- Appointments to the board
- Re-election
- Directors' remuneration level and make-up of remuneration
- Relations with shareholders
- Accountability and audit.

### *Key Recommendations*

- Directors are required to review all internal controls, including financial, operational, compliance and risk management.
- The board reports to shareholders on remuneration.
- A significant proportion of each executive's remuneration package should take the form of performance-related remuneration.

---

[5] *Combined Code on Corporate Governance* (1998; revised 2003 and 2008).

- The annual report must identify and name independent non-executive directors.
- When designing incentive schemes, challenging performance criteria should always be included.
- The majority of the audit committee and the entire remuneration committee should be made up of independent NEDs.

## The Higgs Report (January 2003)[6]

### Key Area of Focus

- Role of the non-executive director

The Higgs Report focuses directly on the role and effectiveness of non-executive directors in promoting company performance as well as issues of accountability.

### Key Recommendations

- At least half of the board should be independent NEDs.
- The roles of chairman and chief executive should be separate, with distinct responsibilities.
- The role of the NED is clarified and includes responsibility for scrutinising the performance of the executive management team and ensuring that financial controls and systems of risk management are robust and defensible.
- Board committees run by NEDs, including a nomination committee, remuneration committee and audit committee, should be utilised.
- Proposals should be aimed at reinforcing the independence of NEDs (e.g. no significant shareholdings or options over shares in the company) and their suitability.
- There should be increased formality regarding the appointment and selection of NEDs and suggestions for broadening the pool of candidates.

---

[6] *Review of the Role and Effectiveness of Non-executive Directors* (Department of Trade and Industry, 2003).

- Guidance on the prospective liabilities of NEDs is necessary, aimed at limiting exposure by emphasising that NEDs have less detailed knowledge of the company's affairs.
- Companies should provide director and officer (D&O) insurance.

## Smith Report (January 2003)[7]

### *Key Area of Focus*

- Audit committees

### *Key Recommendations*

- The audit committee should be comprised of at least three members, all of whom should be independent NEDs.
- At least one member should have significant, recent and relevant financial experience.
- The role of the audit committee is clarified to include monitoring the integrity of the financial statements, reviewing financial reporting judgements and reviewing the company's internal audit function and financial controls.
- The audit committee is also responsible for making recommendations to the board concerning the appointment of the external auditor and for monitoring the external auditor's independence, objectivity and effectiveness.
- The audit committee should develop and implement policy on the engagement of the external auditor to supply non-audit services.

## The Combined Code (Revised July 2003)[8]

*The Combined Code on Corporate Governance* (2003) replaces the 1998 version to reflect recent developments, in particular the *Higgs Report* and the *Smith Report*.

---

[7] *Audit Committees: Combined Code Guidance* (FRC, 2003).
[8] *The Combined Code on Corporate Governance* (FRC, 2003).

147

The Code's overall aim is to enhance board effectiveness and to improve investor confidence by raising standards of corporate governance. Its main features are as follows:

- New definitions of the role of the board, the chairman and the non-executive directors (NEDs).
- More open and rigorous procedures for the appointment of directors.
- Formal evaluation of the performance of boards, committees and individual directors, enhanced induction and more professional development of NEDs.
- At least half the board in larger listed companies to be independent NEDs, with a definition of the independence of NEDs.
- The separation of the roles of the chairman and the chief executive to be reinforced.
- A veto on a chief executive going on to become chairman of the same company.
- Closer relationships between the chairman, the senior independent director, NEDs and major shareholders.
- A strengthened role for the audit committee in monitoring the integrity of the company's financial reporting, reinforcing the independence of the external auditor and reviewing the management of financial and other risks.
- Modification of the Code's structure to include not only main 'principles' and 'provisions' but also 'supporting principles', allowing companies greater flexibility in how they implement the Code.
- The board's chair to be able to chair the nomination committee.
- Clarification of the roles of the chairman and the senior independent director, emphasising the chairman's role in providing leadership to the NEDs and in the communication of shareholders' views to the board.
- For smaller listed companies (below the FTSE 350), relaxation of the rule on the number of independent non-executives to "at least two" instead of "at least 50 per cent".
- Particularly rigorous review, rather than special explanation, when NEDs are re-elected beyond six years.

# Walker Review (2009)[9]

## *Key Areas of Focus*

- Board size, composition and qualification
- Functioning of the board and evaluation of its performance
- The role of institutional shareholders
- Governance of risk
- Remuneration.

## *Key Recommendations*

- Board-level risk committees to be chaired by a NED. Risk committee report to be separate within annual report and accounts.
- Risk committee to be separate from audit committee.
- Increased powers to risk committee to scrutinise and block transactions.
- Annual re-election of the chairman.
- Increased disclosure of executives' remuneration.
- Increased time commitment from NEDs and the chairman. Non-executives to spend 50% more time on the job.
- Chairman should bring substantial industry experience and record of leadership and, if it is a major bank, should give two-thirds of his or her working time to the board.
- Remuneration committee to oversee pay of executives not on the board.
- To facilitate senior management retention, short-term bonuses should be paid over a period of three years, with not more than one-third paid in the first year.
- Increased role for institutional shareholders to engage in and support long-term performance.
- Board should undertake full, formal and rigorous evaluation of performance every two to three years.
- FRC to create a 'Stewardship Code' for institutional investors, with fund managers signifying their commitment to such a code.
- Increased public disclosure about salary of high-paid executives.

---

[9] *A review of corporate governance in UK banks and other financial industry entities: Final recommendations* (26 November 2009).

- If the non-binding resolution on a remuneration committee report attracts less than 75% of the total votes cast, the chairman of the remuneration committee should not stand for re-election to the board in the following year, irrespective of his or her normal appointment term.
- More power for remuneration committees to scrutinise organisation-wide pay rates.

## The UK Corporate Governance Code 2010 (Revised 2012)[10]

### *Key Areas of Focus*

- Establishes standards under five principles:
  - Board leadership
  - Accountability
  - Effectiveness
  - Remuneration
  - Relations with shareholders.

### *Key Recommendations*

**Leadership:**

- Every company should be headed by an effective board.
- Clear division of responsibilities at head of company between the running of the board (i.e. chairman) and executive responsible for running the company (i.e. the chief executive).
- Chairman is responsible for leadership and effectiveness of the board.
- NEDs should constructively challenge and help develop proposals on strategy.

**Effectiveness:**

- Board and its committees should have the appropriate mix of skills, experience, independence and knowledge of the company to enable them to carry out their duties effectively.
- There should be a formal, rigorous and transparent procedure for the appointment of new directors to the board.

---

[10] *The UK Corporate Governance Code* (FRC, 2010; revised 2012).

- Directors should allocate sufficient time to the company to discharge their responsibilities effectively.
- Directors should receive induction on joining the board and should regularly update their skills and knowledge.
- The board should be supplied in a timely manner with information in a form and of a quality appropriate to enable it to discharge its duties.
- The board should undertake a formal and rigorous annual evaluation of its own performance and that of its committees and individual directors.
- All directors should be submitted for re-election at regular intervals, subject to continued satisfactory performance.

## Accountability:

- The board should provide fair, balanced and understandable annual reports.
- The board is responsible for assessing risks it is willing to take in order to achieve strategic goals and for maintaining sound risk management.
- The board should establish formal arrangements for considering how to apply corporate reporting, risk management and internal control systems.

## Remuneration:

- Remuneration of directors should be sufficient to attract, retain and motivate, but should not be more than is necessary for this purpose. A proportion of directors' remuneration should be linked to corporate and individual performance.
- There should be a formal and transparent policy for fixing remuneration packages and directors should not be involved in deciding their own remuneration.

## Relations with shareholders:

- There should be a dialogue with shareholders based on mutual understanding of objectives and the board is responsible for this dialogue taking place.
- Board should use the AGM to communicate with investors and encourage their participation.

# The UK Stewardship Code 2010 (Revised 2012)[11]

## *Key Areas of Focus*

- *The UK Stewardship Code* applies to firms who manage assets on behalf of institutional shareholders.
- Adopts a 'comply or explain' approach.

## *Key Recommendations*

- Institutional investors should:
  - publicly disclose their policy on how they will discharge their stewardship responsibilities;
  - have a robust policy to manage conflicts of interest in relation to stewardship;
  - monitor investee companies;
  - give clear guidelines on when and how they will escalate stewardship activities;
  - be willing to act collectively with other investors when appropriate;
  - have a clear policy on voting and disclosure of voting activity;
  - report periodically on their stewardship and voting activities.

# Irish Corporate Governance Annex[12]

In addition to *The UK Corporate Governance Code*, the Irish Stock Exchange requires Irish listed companies to comply with, or explain against, the recommendations outlined below.

## *Key Recommendations*

- Companies should outline the rationale for the size and composition of their board. Where less than half the board is composed of NEDs, the company should give a reasonable explanation for this. The annual report should give a description of the skills, expertise and experience of directors.

---

[11] *The UK Stewardship Code* (FRC, 2010; revised 2012).
[12] Irish Stock Exchange, *Main Securities Market Listing Rules and Admission to Trading Rules*, Appendix 4, "Irish Corporate Governance Annex" (ISE, 2011).

- Companies should provide an explanation of the process followed by the nomination committee in identifying a pool of candidates and selecting and recommending each candidate. If an external search agency has been used in the process, this should also be stated.
- Companies should state the objectives and scope of the board evaluation review and the methodology used.
- The annual report should include the general policy for board renewal and the factors it took into account when determining when a director should be considered independent.
- The annual report should include a meaningful description of the work carried out by the audit committee, in relation to risk management, and not merely recycle the committee's terms of reference.
- The company should provide clear and meaningful description of its remuneration policy, including details of bonuses, vesting periods for shares and share options.

## Governance Code for Credit Institutions and Insurance Undertakings[13]

### Key Areas of Focus

- Minimum statutory requirements for the governance of banks and insurance companies.
- Provisions in relation to the number of NEDs on the board, the role and responsibility of the chairman and directors, and the operations of board committees.
- Outlines the governance requirements for the boards of banks and insurance companies, with additional requirements for the boards of 'high impact' institutions. These are designated by the Central Bank.

### Key Recommendations

- Designated 'high impact' institutions must have a minimum of seven directors, with a minimum of five in all others.

---

[13] *Governance Code for Credit Institutions and Insurance Undertakings* (Central Bank of Ireland, 2010).

- The role of chief executive and chairman must be separated.
- Financial institutions must have both an audit and a risk committee.
- Requirements on the role and number of independent NEDs.
- Limits on the number of directorships a director may hold in other companies, to ensure they comply with the expected demands of board membership.
- If an individual has been chief executive, executive director or a member of senior management, he or she is prohibited from acting as chairman of that institution for at least five years.
- Annual confirmation of compliance must be submitted to the Central Bank of Ireland, along with other considerable documentation requirements, including a risk-averse remuneration policy.
- The board is required to understand the risks to which the institution is exposed and shall develop a statement of risk appetite for the institution.
- The chief executive's position must be reviewed every five years, the chairman's annually and board membership is required to be reviewed every three years.

## Companies Bill 2012

### Key Areas of Focus

- Seeks to consolidate and simplify 16 previous Companies Acts, dating from 1963 to 2012, into one statute, completely reorganising and reforming Irish company law.
- Changes in:
  - single director companies
  - company constitutions
  - full and unlimited capacity
  - AGMs
  - director's duties (see **Chapter 4**, section on Directors' Statutory Duties)
  - offences
  - mergers
  - the incorporation process (simplified).

## *Key Recommendations*

### Focus on the private company:

- The new Act places the private company limited by shares (LTD), which comprises approximately 90% of Irish companies, at the centre of company law.
- The LTD will be limited by shares, not guarantee, and will have "full and unlimited capacity", abolishing the doctrine of *ultra vires* and the need for an objects clause.
- The LTD will not be allowed to issue securities and will only require a one-document constitution, doing away with Articles of Association and the Memorandum.
- The LTD may have only one single director and directors' duties will be codified and simplified. The company must also have a Company Secretary.
- Private companies will now be able to engage in mergers and divisions.
- Many of the provisions typically set out in a company's Articles of Association will become incorporated into the new Act, requiring companies to only set out *exceptions* to the norm in their constitutions.

### Simplification:

- The requirement to hold a physical AGM with members attending in person is dispensed with; an AGM can be held by written resolution of the members.
- Offences under the Bill are categorised on a scale of 1 to 4, with clearly specified punishments for those found guilty.
- A summary approval procedure (SAP) will allow the LTD to conduct certain procedures without the need for High Court approval, such as financial assistance, reduction of capital or loans to directors.

### Other types of company:

- Parts 1 to 15 of the new Act are concerned with the LTD. Parts 16 to 25 deal with other types of company, such as the PLC, designated activity company (DAC), companies limited by guarantee (CLG) and unlimited companies.

- The DAC is similar to the LTD but must have an objects clause, Memorandum and Articles of Association.
- The PLC must have at least two directors and is the only company able to issue shares to the public.
- The CLG does not have share capital and is the method commonly used by sports or clubs and charities.
- There will be three types of unlimited company: private unlimited companies with a share capital; public unlimited companies with a share capital; and public unlimited companies without a share capital.

## Charities Act 2009

### Key Areas of Focus

- Ensuring greater accountability
- Protecting against fraudulent abuse of charitable status
- Enhancing public trust, confidence and transparency in charities and their trustees

### Key Recommendations

- The Act provides a definition of charitable purposes.
- Creation of a new Charities Regulatory Authority to ensure compliance with legal obligations and to encourage better administration.
- Creation of a Register of Charities in which all charities must register.
- It will be an offence for any organisation that is not a registered charity to present itself to the public as one.
- Submission of annual activity reports to the new Authority.
- Creation of a Charities Appeals Tribunal.
- Updating of the law in relation to fundraising.
- Statutory accounting and auditing obligations imposed on charities not incorporated under the Companies Act.
- Consultative panels to assist the Authority and to ensure effective consultation with stakeholders.
- Charities that are not companies must meet specific financial reporting requirements.

# EU Green Paper – The EU Corporate Governance Framework[14]

## Key Areas of Focus

- Board of directors: NEDs should have diverse skills, appropriate experience and be able to commit sufficient time.
- Shareholders: more active shareholders, interest in sustainable returns and long-term performance.
- How to apply the 'comply or explain approach': a 2009 study[15] has shown that the quality of explanation published by companies departing from the corporate governance codes recommendations is, in the majority of cases, not satisfactory.
- Should the EU have a differentiated approach to account for different types and sizes of company?
- Should the EU take action on corporate governance in unlisted companies?

## Key Recommendations

**Enhance transparency:**

- Proposal to strengthen disclosure requirements in relation to board diversity and risk management.
- Improving quality of corporate reporting, especially the explanations given under 'comply or explain'.
- Initiative to improve visibility of shareholdings in the EU.
- Initiative on disclosure of voting and engagement policies and institutional investors' voting records.

**Engage shareholders:**

- Improve transparency on remuneration of directors and give shareholders right to vote on these policies.
- Improve shareholder control over related-party transactions.
- Improve transparency of conflict-of-interest frameworks.

---

[14] EU Green Paper COM(2011) 164 final Brussels, 5.4.2011.
[15] Study on Monitoring and Enforcement Practices in Corporate Governance in the Member States (http://ec.europa.eu/internal_market/company/docs/ecgforum/studies/comply-or-explain-090923_en.pdf).

- Develop guidance regarding the engagement of long-term investors and the company.
- Encourage development of transnational employee share ownership.

**Cross-border operations:**

- Assess need for initiative on cross-border transfer of companies' registered offices.
- Assess need to revise rules on cross-border mergers.
- Consider need for a cross-border divisional framework.
- Explore ways to improve administrative and regulatory framework for SMEs, follow up on proposal for European private limited company.
- Improve information available on groups of companies and recognition of 'group interest' concept.

**Codification** Plans to merge and restate a number of major EU company law Directives.

# The UK Corporate Governance Code 2014

## *Key Areas of Focus*

- Improving the quality of information investors receive about the long-term health and strategy of listed companies.
- Requirement to include a 'viability statement'.
- Remuneration of key executives to be designed to promote the long-term success of the company, raising the bar for risk management.

## *Key Recommendations*

**Going concern, risk management and internal control:**

- Companies should state whether they consider it appropriate to adopt the going-concern basis of accounting and identify any material uncertainties with regard their ability to continue to do so.
- Companies should robustly assess their principal risks and explain how they are being managed or mitigated.

- Companies should state whether they believe they will be able to continue in operation and meet their liabilities taking account of their current position and principal risks, and specify the period covered by this statement and why they consider it appropriate. It is expected that the period assessed will be significantly longer than 12 months.
- Companies should monitor their risk management and internal control systems and, at least annually, carry out a review of their effectiveness, and report on that review in the annual report.
- Companies can choose where to put the risk and viability disclosures. If placed in the Strategic Report, directors will be covered by the 'safe harbour' provisions in the Companies Act 2006 (UK).

**Remuneration:**

- Greater emphasis be placed on ensuring that remuneration policies are designed with the long-term success of the company in mind, and that the lead responsibility for doing so rests with the remuneration committee.
- Companies should put in place arrangements that will enable them to recover or withhold variable pay when appropriate to do so, and should consider appropriate vesting and holding periods for deferred remuneration.

**Shareholder engagement:**

- Companies should explain when publishing general meeting results how they intend to engage with shareholders when a significant percentage of them have voted against any resolution.

**Other issues:**

- The FRC has also highlighted the importance of the board's role in establishing the 'tone from the top' of the company in terms of its culture and values. The directors should lead by example in order to encourage good behaviours throughout the organisation.

# A2.

## Corporate Governance Checklists

- Introduction
- Improving Board Logistics
- Typical Agenda
- Board Papers
- Approving Board Minutes
- Boardroom Communications
- Utilising Internal Resources
- Developing Strategy in the Boardroom
- Boards of Start-ups
- Family/closely held Boards

## Introduction

This appendix provides a series of useful checklists as a resource for improving all aspects of board productivity. *Note*: the questions and points in each checklist are not exhaustive and may need to be tailored to the stage of life and complexity of the company.

## Improving Board Logistics

- Who is responsible for writing your board and committee meeting agendas? How are the agendas reviewed before being finalised?
- Does your board evaluate the effectiveness of the board meeting agendas as part of the overall process of evaluation?
- Does your board allocate time effectively for each item on the agenda? How many minutes go on basic administrative procedures, presentations and actual board discussion?
- Are agenda items or discussions regularly cut short at the end of board meetings due to lack of time? How could this be addressed in your schedule setting?
- How much time do 'AOB' (any other business) agenda items take up in your board meetings?
- Would non-executive directors (NEDs) be willing to keep a log for a month or two on the total time they devote to your board? Do any NEDs feel the board meetings could be used more effectively?
- How much informal discussion time does your board meeting system offer between directors and managers?
- Has your board reviewed its current meeting schedule recently (bimonthly, quarterly, one-day, half-day, etc.)? Is the current meeting set-up the most effective?
- Is there a person or office responsible for board meeting and administration logistics? Has this been formally set up with written duties?

## Typical Agenda

The typical agenda for a board meeting should include the following:

- Approval of the minutes of the last board meeting and matters arising
- The chief executive's report including other function reports such as HR, ICT, etc.

- The finance director's report
- Review of ongoing projects and operational issues
- Operational, procedural and compliance issues
- New initiatives
- Business outlook
- Progress against the strategic plan (quarterly)
- Any other business
- Date of next meeting.

## Board Papers

The papers required for a board meeting could include:

- The agenda
- Minutes of the previous meeting
- The chief executive's report, including other functional reports such as HR, ICT etc.
- Management accounts and the finance director's report
- Papers relating to specific agenda items
- Committee reports
- Corporate and business plans.

## Approving Board Minutes

- Look over minutes from the previous board meeting. The minutes should record the meeting in such a way that should a decision subsequently be scrutinised, it can be 'stood over' by the board.
- How closely do you as a director personally review minutes of the previous board meeting before voting to approve them?
- Have there ever been cases where the wording of an issue recorded in the minutes is not how you recall it originally being phrased?
- Is director satisfaction with company procedures included in the board evaluation process (see **Chapter 7**)?
- What administrative process do the minutes follow, and do final minutes always go to the full board for approval?
- Check your latest board minutes for qualifying phrases, such as "concerns were raised" and "extensive discussion followed", to ensure that the minutes reflect accurately the discussion that took place.

## Boardroom Communications

- How long does it take to read through the board's minutes? Does the board need to adopt a more concise approach to minute taking?
- While reading through the minutes, try viewing the material with the fresh eye of an outside analyst. Is there enough material here for a knowledgeable outsider to obtain a good understanding of the company? Are there any obvious omissions or useless material?
- Consider drawing up a list of staff members with whom new directors should meet.
- If an index page is included with the board papers, consider adding a checkbox next to each listing and asking directors to tick items they consider most useful (or least useful). Also, ask for comments on further material that they would like to receive.
- Ensure that the quality, quantity and timeliness of information that goes to the board are included in your board and chief executive evaluation plans.
- For a new director, consider designating a current member of the board to act as a short-term 'mentor', introducing him or her to key people and answering his or her questions.
- How effective is the company's internal process for assembling board papers?
- What proportion of the time at a typical meeting of your board is taken up by presentations to the board? If it is too high, then there may not be sufficient time left for discussion and debate.
- On average, how long before a board meeting do the board papers reach directors? Do you have a firm target deadline on this?

## Utilising Internal Resources

- Have your board and chief executive agreed on a policy for board contacts with the executive management team? Do you as a director feel comfortable making such contacts?
- What are the key areas of the company that are most crucial to success in your business (finance, technology, sales, legal, manufacturing, HR, etc.)? Does your board have regular two-way contact with managers in the most important of these areas?

- Does the performance evaluation plan for the managers of these areas include an assessment of their relationship with the board?
- Does your finance director know which financial reports your board considers most important to do its job (and is your board receiving them)?
- Ask the head of your company's key administrative areas (legal, internal audit, etc.) to prepare brief reports suggesting ways they could provide more value to the board.
- Does your board contain talent among its NEDs that could serve as the board's 'liaison' with these offices, e.g. a solicitor/barrister to liaise with the legal office and someone with specific finance background to liaise with the finance director, etc.? Should this be a consideration in your future board recruiting?
- How the company's internal resources better help the board with its own internal functions (evaluation, succession planning, administration, etc.).
- How often do members of the executive management team and other managers participate in board meetings? Do your directors find their presentations useful?
- Is the information you receive from internal resources clear and informative?
- Are your board committees making the best use of internal resources?

## Developing Strategy in the Boardroom

- Review your company's current strategic plan. How much board input went into shaping it? Are there specific areas of weakness your board needs to address?
- Ask individual directors to prioritise the elements of your strategic plan. Do most have the same view?
- Does your board regularly review company strategic plans for such items as changes in the external environment or warning signs of failure?
- Review the company's overall strategic planning process in a flowchart. Where is the board of directors involved?
- Establish who of the current board members has strategy planning skills, as well as career backgrounds in specific areas vital to the long-term strategy of the company.

- Review your board's experience in managing significant events (insolvency or trading difficulties, major mergers or spin-offs, share splits, etc.).
- Develop a brief list of the board's duties or decisions that have been particularly difficult to resolve. Could any of these benefit from holding a board 'away day' on the topic?
- Have any board members participated in board 'away days' with other companies and what suggestions do they have on ways to improve yours?

## Boards of Start-ups

- Do NEDs hold a strong equity interest in the new company, either as initial investors or by purchasing stock out of their own personal finances?
- Was the initial group of directors selected for specific strategic reasons (as opposed to happenstance or politics)? Can you name the strategic role for each?
- Can each member of your start-up board finish the following statement: "My contribution on this board will be ..." in a way that would satisfy the other members as to the value he or she adds?
- How many members are on your board? (Five to seven is probably ideal for a start-up board.)
- Does the board have a plan for its own development to meet the company's needs as it grows?
- Does the board have its own terms of reference, addressing matters such as size, board compensation, tenure, committees and independence?
- Within the start-up board, are founders, capital representatives and managers in general agreement on strategic goals and targets, and timelines for their achievement?
- Does at least one director have leadership experience with a company larger than your own?
- For IPO (initial public offering) companies, how many board members have previous experience with an IPO?
- Are there any members of your board whose resignation would have serious repercussions for the company?

## Family/closely held Boards

- What are the advantages and disadvantages that your family ownership structure brings to your company's governance?
- How many 'independent' board members are there and is this number sufficient to make an impact?
- How formal are your board meetings? How often do they take place? How long do they last?
- Does the board discuss succession planning with the chief executive on at least a yearly basis? Does a firm, accepted succession plan exist?
- Has your company had any problems with the concerns of minority shareholders?
- How many of your present directors serve as outside directors on other boards?
- If your board currently lacks outside talent, try drawing up profiles of potential directors who could make a valuable addition to it.
- Does your board have 'constituent' members who tend to represent a segment of the family?
- Does your company have a long-term estate plan that deals with inheritance issues, division of assets, tax concerns and so on? Is it generally supported by all?
- Has the company considered having a family or an external expert advisory board?

# A3.

# Matters Reserved for the Board

- **Introduction**
- **Values, Future Direction and Management**
- **Capital Structure**
- **Financial Oversight and Internal Controls**
- **Contractual Obligations**
- **Shareholder and Stakeholder Management**
- **Board Membership, Appointments and Removals**
- **Compensation**
- **Corporate Governance**
- **Board and Company Policies**

# Introduction

In this appendix we set out a model schedule of matters and decisions reserved for the board, outlining decisions that need to be elevated by the executive management team to the board. What should be decided or not decided by the executive management team will depend on the materiality and impact of the decision on the company.

## Values, Future Direction and Management

- Overall responsibility for the leadership of the company, establishing the company's ethics and values and setting the tone from the top.
- Reviewing and approving the company's mission, vision, goals and strategic objectives.
- Reviewing and approving the company's annual business plan and budget.
- Monitoring performance against the company's strategic plan, annual business plan and budgets.
- Approving capital expenditure budgets and their ongoing monitoring.
- Ensuring that the company is fit for purpose in terms of:
  ○ an executive management team with the appropriate skills and experience;
  ○ strategic, business planning and management systems and supporting processes;
  ○ risk management and internal control systems.
- Approving, mergers and acquisitions, joint ventures and expansion internationally or closing down operations.
- Management structures.

## Capital Structure

- Changes relating to the increase or reduction of capital, share issues of all types, and share option schemes.

- Major changes to the company's capital and shareholding structure.
- Issuance of new debt or bonds.
- Changes to the company's listing on a stock exchange, if it is a PLC, or its legal structures.
- Approval of any equity returned to the shareholders.

## Financial Oversight and Internal Controls

- Approval of:
  - quarterly or half-yearly reports for PLCs, and any announcement in relation to results for the public or investor community;
  - annual statutory accounts, including the directors' compliance statement;
  - major financial policies, such as dividends, investment policies, etc.;
  - significant changes in accounting policies or practices;
  - material unbudgeted capital or expenditure overruns, banking borrowings, overdrafts over agreed limits and security arrangements;
  - specified financial instruments that carry risk outside certain thresholds;
- Ensuring that there are the appropriate and robust systems of internal control and risk management.

## Contractual Obligations

- Approval of major capital projects, such as purchase of land, ICT systems, new facilities and their subsequent oversight and monitoring.
- Investments that are material or strategically significant, such as acquisitions or disposals of fixed assets, intellectual property, subsidiaries, shareholdings in other companies (above agreed thresholds).
- Investments/contracts that are not in the ordinary course of business.
- Major investments in the voting shares of any company within agreed parameters or the making of any takeover offer.

## Shareholder and Stakeholder Management

- Ongoing and consistent engagement with shareholders and stakeholders based on the mutual understanding of the company's objectives.
- Approval of resolutions and supporting documentation for presentation to shareholders at a general meeting.
- Approval of all circulars, prospectuses, listing particulars and press releases concerning matters decided by the board.

## Board Membership, Appointments and Removals

- Changes to the structure, size and composition of the board.
- Succession planning for the board and senior management.
- Appointments to the board.
- Selection of the chairman, senior independent director, chairs of board committees and the chief executive.
- Membership of board committees.
- Appointment or removal of the Company Secretary.
- Appointment, reappointment or removal of the external auditor.
- Appointments to boards of subsidiaries or joint ventures.
- Removal of any director in breach of the terms of their appointment.
- Removal of the chief executive.
- Approval of external directorships for the chief executive or other executive directors.

## Compensation

- Developing and approving the remuneration policy for the chief executive, Company Secretary and other senior executives.
- Developing and approving the remuneration of NEDs, subject to the Articles of the company/company constitution, with shareholder approval as appropriate.
- Introduction or changes to share incentive schemes for shareholder approval.

## Corporate Governance

- Division of the roles and responsibilities between the chairman, the chief executive and other executive directors (this should be in writing and agreed by the board).
- Approval of the delegated levels of authority, including the chief executive's authority limits and other members of the executive management team.
- Establishing board committees, approving their terms of reference and any authorities where appropriate and reviewing on a regular basis.
- Receiving activities reports from board committees in a specified format.
- Undertaking a formal and annual review of the board's own performance, its committees and of individual directors. An external review should take place at least every three years.
- Assessing the independence of NEDs, to be reported in the annual report.
- Receiving feedback on the views of the company's shareholders and stakeholders, ensuring that they are communicated to the board as a whole on a regular basis.
- Adjudicating on conflicts of interest where appropriate.

## Board and Company Policies

- A critical role of the board is in setting policies that will set the standards within which the company will operate. The role of the board is to review and approve relevant policies, including:
  - The Code of Conduct
  - Share Dealing Code
  - Whistle-blowing Policy
  - Health & Safety Policy
  - Environment and Sustainability Policy
  - Communications Policy
  - Investor Relations Policy
  - Corporate Social Responsibility (CSR) Policy; and
  - Charitable and Political Donations Policy.

It should be noted that the executive management team will also be involved in more detailed policy development, such as those related to internet access during work, for example.

- Other items requiring board approval would include:
  - ○ Approval of the appointment of the company's principal professional advisors.
  - ○ Litigation matters above agreed thresholds (i.e. where legal costs are likely to exceed an agreed limit).
  - ○ Directors' and officers' (D&O) liability insurance and policy in relation to indemnification of directors where the liability is not covered by the D&O insurance.
  - ○ Changes related to any defined benefit or defined contribution pension scheme where it may have a material impact on the company and any changes of trustees.
  - ○ Any other decision likely to have a material impact on the company.

# A4.

# Sample Terms of Reference for Board Committees and the Executive Management Committee

- **Audit Committee: Sample Terms of Reference**
- **Nomination Committee: Sample Terms of Reference**
- **Remuneration Committee: Sample Terms of Reference**
- **Risk Committee: Sample Terms of Reference**
- **Sample Charter for an Executive Management Committee**

# AUDIT COMMITTEE: SAMPLE TERMS OF REFERENCE

These sample terms of reference are intended as the basis for drawing up the terms of reference for an audit committee. The level of detail and particular emphasis required will be specific to each company and will have to be carefully considered by the audit committee before bringing to the board for approval.

## Purpose

- The purpose of the Audit Committee is to provide formal and transparent arrangements for considering how to apply financial and internal reporting principles in accordance with best practice or a relevant standard or code and to maintain an appropriate relationship with the company's auditors.

## Membership

- The board shall appoint the committee and all [three][1] members of the committee shall be non-executive directors (NEDs). At least one member of the committee should have recent and relevant financial experience. The quorum for the committee shall be [two] members. The board will also appoint the chairman who should be also be a NED.
- The Company Secretary shall act as the secretary to the audit committee.

## Attendance at Meetings

- Only the members of the audit committee are entitled to attend audit committee meetings. Others may attend committee meetings at the invitation of the committee. Such persons could include the chairman of the board, non-executive members of the

---

[1] Square brackets contain recommendations in line with best practice but which may need to be changed to suit the circumstances of the particular organisation, or excluded where not relevant.

board, the chief executive, the CFO, representatives of the external auditors, the head of internal audit, etc.

- There should be at least one meeting per year where the audit committee meets the external auditors/internal auditors without any executive management team members present.

## Meetings

- The committee shall meet no less than [four] times a year, to coincide with the company's financial reporting cycle. The head of internal audit or the external auditors can request a meeting with the committee, if required.
- The quorum necessary for the transaction of business shall be [two] independent non-executive directors.
- The committee shall meet at least [twice] a year and at such other times as the chairman of the committee shall think appropriate or necessary.
- Meetings of the committee shall be called by the secretary of the committee at the request of any member.
- Unless otherwise agreed by all members of the committee, notice of each meeting confirming the venue, time and date, together with an agenda and all relevant papers, should normally be circulated to each member of the committee, and to any other person required to attend, at least [five] working days prior to the date of the meeting.
- Decisions of the committee will be by majority vote. In the event of a tied vote, the chairman will have a casting vote.

## Duties

The duties of the committee shall include the following:

### *Financial Reporting*

- Review and challenge, as appropriate, the actions and judgements of the executive management team in relation to all matters related to the annual and interim financial statements, interim reporting, preliminary announcements, etc., before submission to and approval by the board and before clearance by the external auditors. Attention should also be paid to:

- any change to accounting policies;
- matters requiring a significant element of judgement;
- significant adjustments;
- clarity of required disclosures;
- the going concern assumption;
- compliance with relevant accounting standards and other legal requirements.

- Consider any other matters as defined by the board.

## *External Audit*

- Oversee the relationship with the company's external auditors.
- Consider and make recommendations on the appointment, reappointment or removal of the external auditors.
- Approve the terms of engagement of and the fees to be paid to the external auditors for audit services.
- Ensure that the qualifications, skills, experience and the resources, as well as the independence of the external auditors, are sufficient for them to carry out their role.
- Meet with the external auditors to discuss the nature and scope of the audit before it commences.
- Discuss with the external auditors the findings of their work and any major issues that have been identified during the audit which need to be addressed by the audit committee and/or brought to the attention of the board.
- Review the letter of representation before it is placed before the board for consideration and approval.
- Review at the end of the audit process the effectiveness of the process and any changes that may be required for the audit in the following year.
- Review the external auditors' management letter to ensure that, subject to the audit committee's agreement, its recommendations are acted on.
- Ensure that the independence of the auditor is not compromised by the provision of non-audit services and, if it is, recommend to the board an appropriate course of action.

## Internal Audit and Internal Controls

- Review the effectiveness of the company's internal control framework and processes.
- Consider on a regular basis where there is a need for a formal internal audit function.
- Monitor and review the effectiveness of the internal audit function and to make sure it is adequately resourced.
- Review the internal audit programme and the internal audit reports to ensure that the function has the requisite degree of independence to fulfil its role.
- Review with senior management the appointment and removal of the head of the internal audit, as appropriate.
- Ensure that the head of internal audit has the appropriate access to the chairman of the board and the chairman of the audit committee and that it is accountable to the audit committee.
- Receive regular reports from the head of internal audit against the agreed work plan and other matters as appropriate.
- Assess management responsiveness to external or internal audit findings and recommendations.
- Review the procedures for detecting fraud and whistle-blowing in relation to all aspects of the company's operations.
- Review internal audit and management reports on the integrity of the systems for internal financial control and financial reporting.

## Reporting

- The chairman of the audit committee should attend the board meeting at which the statutory accounts are approved.
- The audit committee should review its terms of reference on an annual basis, make any changes and recommend them to the board.
- The annual report should contain a report from the audit committee on how it has discharged its role since the last annual report. It should also note any disagreements between the board and the audit committee that cannot be resolved in the report.
- The chairman of the audit committee should attend the company's AGM and answer any questions on the committee's activities and responsibilities.

## Authority

The committee is authorised by the board to:

- investigate any activity within the agreed terms of reference;
- seek any information it requires from staff;
- obtain outside legal or other professional help at the company's expense.

# NOMINATION COMMITTEE: SAMPLE TERMS OF REFERENCE

These sample terms of reference are intended as the basis for drawing up the terms of reference for a nomination committee. The level of detail and particular emphasis required will be specific to each company and will have to be carefully considered by the nomination committee before bringing to the board for approval.

## Purpose

- The purpose of the nomination committee is to establish a formal, rigorous and transparent process for the appointment of new directors to the board of a company.

## Membership

- The nomination committee has been established as a committee by resolution of the board.
- The chairman and members of the committee shall be appointed by the board. The chair of the company can be chair of the committee except when it is dealing with the appointment of a successor to the current chairman.

- The committee shall comprise at least [three][2] directors, the majority of whom shall be independent non-executive directors.
- Only members of the committee have the right to attend committee meetings. Other individuals may attend committee meetings at the invitation of the committee. Such persons could include the chairman of the board, non-executive members of the board, the chief executive, the CFO, representatives of the external auditors, the head of internal audit, etc.
- Appointments to the committee shall be made by the board for a period of up to three years, which may be extended for further periods of up to three years, provided the appointee (director) still meets the criteria for membership of the committee.
- In the absence of the chairman of the committee, the members present shall elect one of their number present who would qualify under these terms of reference to be appointed to that position by the board.
- The Company Secretary, or his or her nominee, shall act as the secretary of the committee. Where the Company Secretary is also an executive director, the committee may nominate one of its members to act as secretary for any meeting the committee wishes to hold without executive directors being present.

## Meetings

- The quorum necessary for the transaction of business shall be [two] independent non-executive directors.
- The committee shall meet at least [twice] a year and at such other times as the chairman of the committee shall think appropriate or necessary.
- Meetings of the committee shall be called by the secretary of the committee at the request of any member.
- Unless otherwise agreed by all members of the committee, notice of each meeting, confirming the venue, time and date, together with an agenda and all relevant papers, should normally be circulated to each member of the committee, and to any other person

---

[2] Square brackets contain recommendations in line with best practice but which may need to be changed to suit the circumstances of the particular organisation, or excluded where not relevant.

required to attend, at least [five] working days prior to the date of the meeting.

- Decisions of the committee will be by majority vote. In the event of a tied vote, the chairman will have a casting vote.

## Reporting

- Adequate time should be allowed after committee meetings to enable the committee to consider its discussions, recommendations and any specific actions to be taken. The secretary shall minute the proceedings and resolutions of all committee meetings, as well as the names of those present and in attendance. (Part attendance by members should also be noted.)
- Draft minutes of committee meetings shall be circulated promptly to all members of the committee and, once agreed, to all other members of the board, unless it would be inappropriate to do so.
- The committee chairman shall report to the board on its proceedings after each meeting and make any recommendations as it sees fit. The chair of the committee shall attend the company's AGM to answer any shareholder questions on the committee's activities.
- The committee shall also include in the company's annual report an account of its activities and the process used to appoint directors to the board. If an external search firm was used, it should be identified, as should any connection between that firm and the company.

## Duties of the Committee

- The following duties shall be carried out by the committee for the company and related entities, as appropriate:
  - Regularly review the structure, size and composition of the board and make recommendations to it with regarding any changes that it proposes. This review should also include the skills, knowledge, experience and diversity of the board.
  - Give full consideration to ongoing succession planning for directors and members of the executive team taking into account the future strategic direction of the company and the skills and expertise needed on the board to support this.

185

- Keep under constant review the company's leadership resources, both executive and non-executive, to ensure the company's capability to compete effectively and deliver on its strategy.
- Be fully informed about the strategic issues and related changes affecting the company and the market in which it competes.
- Be responsible for identifying, and nominating for the approval of the board, candidates to fill board vacancies in line with the company's board rotation policy.
- Evaluate the balance of skills, knowledge, experience and diversity on the board, to assist in defining the role and capabilities required for a particular appointment before any appointment is made. In identifying suitable candidates the committee shall consider:
  - candidates from a wide range of backgrounds;
  - using open advertising or external search services to assist it in its role;
  - candidates on merit and against documented objective criteria;
  - the benefits of diversity on the board, ensuring that potential candidates have enough time available to devote to the role.
- For the appointment of a chairman, prepare a job specification, including the time commitment expected. A proposed chairman's other major commitments should be disclosed to the board before any appointment is considered and any changes to the chairman's commitments should be reported to the board as and when they arise.
- Prior to the appointment of a director, the proposed appointee should be required to disclose any business interests, current or future, that may result in a conflict of interests.
- Ensure that prior to accepting appointment to the board, NEDs receive a formal letter of appointment setting out clearly what is expected of them in terms of time commitment, committee work and involvement outside board meetings, so that they can consider it before formal acceptance of the role.
- Review the results of the annual board performance evaluation process that relate to the board's composition. (*Note*: an external and objective evaluation of the board should take place every three years at least.)
- Review annually the time required from NEDs. The performance evaluation process should be used to assess whether NEDs are devoting enough time to fulfil their duties.

- The committee shall also make recommendations to the board concerning the following:
  - Developing succession plans for executive and non-executive directors, particularly for the key roles of chairman and chief executive.
  - Identifying suitable candidates for the role of senior independent director.
  - Identifying members for all board committees in consultation with the chairman of each of those committees.
  - Reappointment of any NED at the conclusion of their specified term of office, having given due regard to their performance and ability to continue to contribute to the board in the light of knowledge, skills, experience and the time commitment required.
  - The re-election by shareholders of directors under any annual re-election provisions of relevant codes or the retirement by rotation provisions in the company's Articles of Association and the need for the ongoing renewal of the Board (particularly in relation to directors being re-elected for a term beyond six years).
  - Any matters relating to the continuation in office of any director at any time, including the suspension or termination of service of an executive director as an employee of the company subject to the provisions of the law and their service contract.
  - The appointment of any director to executive or other office.

## Other Matters

- The committee shall:
  - have access to sufficient resources in order to carry out its duties, including access to the company secretariat and outside professional assistance, as required;
  - be provided with the appropriate training and information on compensation trends as and when required;
  - give due consideration to laws, regulations or codes that may apply;
  - arrange for an annual review of its own performance, including its terms of reference and recommend any changes it considers necessary to the board for approval.

## Authority

- The committee is authorised by the board to:
  - investigate any activity or state of affairs within its terms of reference;
  - obtain, at the company's expense, outside legal or other professional advice on any matters within its terms of reference;
  - obtain any information required from any officer or staff member. In seeking advice or assistance from any of the company's executives, the committee should ensure that such role is clearly separated from the executive's role within the company.

# REMUNERATION COMMITTEE: SAMPLE TERMS OF REFERENCE

These sample terms of reference are intended as the basis for drawing up the terms of reference for a remuneration committee. The level of detail and particular emphasis required will be specific to each company and will have to be carefully considered by the remuneration committee before bringing to the board for approval.

## Purpose

The purpose of the committee is to establish a formal and transparent process for developing remuneration policy for directors and senior executive management.

## Membership

- The committee has been established as a committee of the board by resolution of the board.
- The members of the committee shall be appointed by the board. The chair of the committee, who should be a non-executive

director (NED), shall be appointed by the board on the nomination of the remuneration committee.

- The committee shall comprise at least [two][3] members, all of whom shall be independent NEDs. The chairman of the board may also serve on the committee as an additional member but not as the chairman.
- Only members of the committee have the right to attend committee meetings. However, other individuals may be invited to attend for all or part of any meeting, as and when appropriate.
- The chief executive has the right to address any meetings of the committee.
- Appointments to the committee shall be made by the board for a period of up to [two] years, extendable by no more than [two] additional [two]-year periods provided that members (other than the chairman of the board, if he or she is a member of the committee) continue to be independent.
- In the absence of the chairman of the committee, the members present shall elect one of their number present who would qualify under these terms of reference to be appointed to that position by the board.
- The Company Secretary or his or her nominee shall act as the secretary of the committee.
- If the Company Secretary is an executive director, the committee may nominate one of its members to act as secretary for meetings the committee wishes to hold without any executive directors present.

## Meetings

- The committee shall meet at least [twice] a year and at such other times as the chairman of the committee shall think appropriate or necessary.
- Meetings of the committee shall be called by the secretary of the committee at the request of any member of the committee.

---

[3] Square brackets contain recommendations in line with best practice but which may need to be changed to suit the circumstances of the particular organisation, or excluded where not relevant.

- Unless otherwise agreed by all members of the committee, notice of each meeting, confirming the venue, time and date, together with an agenda and all relevant documentation, shall normally be circulated to each member of the committee and any other person required to attend no later than [five] working days before the date of the meeting.
- The quorum for meetings of the committee shall be [two] members

## Reporting

- Adequate time should be allowed after committee meetings to enable the committee to consider its discussions, recommendations and any specific actions to be taken. The secretary shall minute the proceedings and resolutions of all meetings of the committee, including the names of those present and in attendance. (Part attendance should also be noted.)
- Draft minutes of committee meetings shall be circulated promptly to committee members and, once agreed, to other members of the board, unless it would be inappropriate to do so.
- The committee shall produce a report of the company's remuneration policy and practices to be included in the annual report and accounts and, if required, ensure that any resolutions are put to the shareholders for approval at the AGM.
- The committee chairman shall report to the board on its proceedings after each meeting and make any recommendations as it sees fit. The chair of the committee shall attend the AGM to answer any shareholder questions on the committee's activities.

## Duties of the Committee

The following duties shall be carried out by the committee for the company and related entities, as appropriate:

- Discuss and agree with the board the broad policy for the remuneration of the chairman of the board, the chief executive, all other executive directors and other members of the executive management team within its terms of reference. The remuneration of NEDs shall be a matter for the executive directors of the board.

No director or senior executive shall be involved in any decisions as to their own remuneration. The committee shall also review and recommend to the board the remuneration of the Company Secretary.

- In determining remuneration policies, take into account all factors that the committee deems necessary, including relevant legal and regulatory requirements, the provisions and recommendations of the relevant codes and associated guidance. The objective of such policies shall be to ensure that members of executive management are provided with the appropriate incentives to encourage enhanced performance both in the short and longer terms and are rewarded for their collective and individual contributions to the company.
- Liaise with the nomination committee to ensure that the remuneration policy of newly appointed executives and NEDs is in line with overall company policy.
- Review the ongoing appropriateness and relevance of remuneration policies within the company and ensure they are market related.
- Within the terms of the agreed policy and in consultation with the chairman and/or chief executive, as appropriate, determine the total individual remuneration package of each executive director, the company chairman and other designated senior executives, including bonuses, pensions, incentive payments and share options or other share awards.
- Obtain reliable, up-to-date information about remuneration in other comparable companies. To help assist it in its work, the committee shall have the authority to appoint remuneration consultants and to commission or purchase any reports, surveys or information which it deems necessary, at the expense of the company and within budgets set by the board.
- Be exclusively responsible for determining the selection criteria, and selecting, appointing and setting the terms of reference for any remuneration consultants who advise the committee.
- Approve the design of, and determine targets for, any performance-related pay schemes operated by the company and approve the total annual payments made under such schemes.
- Review the design of all share-incentive plans for approval by the board and shareholders. For any such plans, determine each year whether awards will be made and, if so, the overall amount

of such awards, the individual awards to executive directors, Company Secretary and other designated senior executives, and the performance targets to be used.

- Determine the policy for, and scope of, pension arrangements, if any, for each executive director and other designated senior executives.
- When setting remuneration policy for directors, review and have regard to pay and employment conditions across the company, especially when determining annual salary increases.
- Review the design of all share incentive plans for approval by the board and shareholders. For all such plans, determine each year whether awards will be made and, if so, the overall amount of such awards, the individual awards to executive directors, Company Secretary and other designated senior executives and the performance targets to be used.
- Ensure that contractual terms on termination, and any payments made, are fair to the individual and the company, that failure is not rewarded and that the duty to mitigate loss is fully recognised.
- Oversee any major changes in employee benefits structures throughout the company and ensure that any changes do not put the company at a competitive disadvantage.
- Agree the policy for authorising claims for expenses from the chairman and directors.
- Work and liaise as necessary with all other board committees.

## Other Matters

The committee shall:

- have access to sufficient resources in order to carry out its duties, including access to the company secretariat and outside professional assistance, as required;
- be provided with the appropriate training and information on compensation trends as and when required;
- give due consideration to laws, regulations or any codes that may apply;
- arrange for an annual review of its own performance, including its terms of reference, and recommend any changes it considers necessary to the board for approval.

## Authority

The committee is authorised by the board to:

- obtain any information required from any officer or staff member. In seeking any advice or assistance from any of the company's executives, the committee should ensure that such role is clearly separated from the executive's role within the company;
- obtain, at the company's expense, outside legal or other professional advice on any matters within its terms of reference;
- select, set the terms of reference for and appoint remuneration consultants at the company's expense;
- commission any reports or surveys it deems necessary to fulfil its obligations;
- investigate any activity or state of affairs within its terms of reference.

# RISK COMMITTEE: SAMPLE TERMS OF REFERENCE

These sample terms of reference are intended as the basis for drawing up the terms of reference for a risk committee. The level of detail and particular emphasis required will be specific to each company and will have to be carefully considered by the risk committee before bringing to the board for approval.

## Purpose

The purpose of the committee is to assist the Board in establishing the company's risk level and risk appetite and to develop the appropriate risk policies to provide direction to the executive management team and staff. Line management have primary responsibility for the management of risk.

## Membership

- The committee has been established as a committee of the board by resolution of the board.

- The members of the committee shall be appointed by the board. The chair of the committee, who should be a non-executive director (NED), shall be appointed by the board on the nomination of the risk committee.
- Members of the committee shall be appointed in consultation with the chairman of the risk committee.
- The committee shall consist of at least [two][4] members, all of whom should be non-executive directors (NEDs) of the company. The chairman of the risk committee must be a director of the company. The activities of the risk committee should involve participation by the chairman of the audit committee. Appointments to the committee shall be for a period of up to [three] years, which may be extended for further periods of up to [three] years, provided the director still meets the criteria for membership of the committee.
- A majority of members of the committee shall be independent NEDs.
- Only members of the committee have the right to attend committee meetings. However, other individuals may be invited to attend all or part of any meeting as and when deemed appropriate and necessary by the board or its risk committee.
- The board shall appoint the committee chairman who shall be a NED.
- In the absence of the chairman of the committee, the members present shall elect one of their number present who would qualify under these terms of reference to be appointed to that position by the board.
- The Company Secretary, or his or her delegate, shall act as the secretary to the risk committee.

## Meetings

- The committee shall meet at least [three] times a year and other times as required.
- Meetings of the committee shall be convened by the secretary of the committee or at the request of any of its members.
- Unless otherwise agreed by all members of the committee, notice of each meeting, confirming the venue, time and date together

---

[4] Square brackets contain recommendations in line with best practice but which may need to be changed to suit the circumstances of the particular organisation, or excluded where not relevant.

with an agenda and all relevant documentation, shall normally be circulated to each member of the committee, and any other person required to attend and all other non-executive directors, no later than [five] working days before the date of the meeting.
- The quorum for meetings of the committee shall be [two] members.

## Reporting

- Adequate time should be allowed after committee meetings to enable the committee to consider its discussions, recommendations and any specific actions to be taken. The secretary shall minute the proceedings and resolutions of all meetings of the committee, including the names of those present and in attendance. (Part attendance should also be noted.)
- Draft minutes of committee meetings shall be circulated promptly to committee members and, once agreed, to all other members of the board, unless it would be inappropriate to do so.
- In addition to their management reporting line to the chief executive, the executive responsible for risk shall have a direct reporting line to the chairman of the committee on matters within the committee's terms of reference.
- The committee shall produce an annual report of the company's risk management policy and practices to be included in the annual report and accounts.
- The committee chairman shall report to the board on its proceedings after each meeting and make any recommendations as it sees fit. The chair of the committee shall attend the AGM to answer any shareholder questions on the committee's activities and responsibilities.
- The committee shall undertake a review of its performance and these terms of reference annually and, if appropriate, make recommendations to the board for approval.

## Duties of the Committee

The duties of the committee shall be to:

- Review the company's appetite for risk and future risk strategy, particularly for economic, capital, liquidity, data protection, reputational and operational risk, and make recommendations on risk appetite to the board.

- Review the principle risk policies for consistency with the company's risk appetite and to approve any significant changes to these policies.
- Review the company's risk profile against its risk appetite and strategy; review the drivers of these changes, if any, in the risk profile and their implications for economic capital and liquidity; review management actions, if any, required in response to these changes in the risk profile and emerging or potential risks; review the company's capability to identify and manage new risk types [in conjunction with the audit committee].
- Review the company's capability to identify and manage new risk types, such as cyber or social media [in conjunction with the audit committee].
- Review the design, completeness and effectiveness of the risk management framework; review the adequacy of concerns raised by staff, or others, regarding possible irregularities in financial reporting or related matters, such as detecting fraud or the prevention of bribery.
- Keep under review the company's overall risk assessment processes that inform the board's decision making, ensuring both qualitative and quantitative metrics are used; review regularly and approve the parameters used in these measures and the methodology adopted.
- Set a standard for the accurate and timely monitoring of large exposures and certain risk types of critical importance.
- Review annually the adequacy and quality of the company's compliance and risk functions. Ensure that it has adequate resources and appropriate access to information to enable it to perform its function effectively. The committee shall also ensure the function has adequate independence and is free from management and other restrictions.
- Assist the audit committee in its review of the adequacy and effectiveness of the company's internal control system, including financial reporting and financial controls.
- Approve the statements to be included in the annual report concerning internal controls and risk management.
- Review reports on any material breaches of risk limits and the adequacy and timeliness of action taken by executive management.
- Review and monitor management's responsiveness to the findings and recommendations of the chief risk officer (CRO).

- Recommend to the board the appointment and/or removal of the CRO.
- Review promptly all reports on the company from the CRO.
- Ensure the CRO shall be given the right of unfettered direct access to the chairman of the board and to the risk committee.

> *Note*: There are certain duties that could be undertaken by either the audit committee or the risk committee and, consequently, there may be some overlap in their duties. The precise allocation of responsibilities should be detailed in the terms of reference for the audit and risk committees, and should be agreed by the board. It is recommended that the board should err on the side of overlapping duties rather than running the risk of gaps occurring.

## Other Matters

The committee shall:

- have access to sufficient resources in order to carry out its duties, including access to the company secretariat and outside professional assistance, as required;
- be provided with the appropriate training and information on risk trends as and when required;
- give due consideration to any laws, regulations or codes that may apply;
- arrange for an annual review of its own performance, including its terms of reference, and recommend any changes it considers necessary to the board for approval.

## Authority

The committee is authorised to:

- investigate, or cause to be investigated, any activity within its terms of reference;
- obtain, at the company's expense, external legal or other professional advice on any matter within its terms of reference where required;

- seek any information it requires from any employee/director of the company in order to perform its duties;
- request the attendance of any employee at a meeting of the committee as and when required.

# SAMPLE CHARTER FOR AN EXECUTIVE MANAGEMENT COMMITTEE

These sample terms of reference are intended as the basis for drawing up the terms of reference for an executive management committee. The level of detail and particular emphasis required will be specific to each company and will have to be carefully considered by the executive management committee before bringing to the board for approval.

## Objectives and Authority

The objective of the executive management committee (EMC) is to support the chief executive in the performance of his or her duties within the authority parameters set by the board. These include:

- development and, subject to board approval, implementation of strategy, business and operational plans, policies and procedures;
- monitoring of day-to day-operational and financial performance;
- identification, evaluation and management of risk;
- prioritisation and allocation of resources across all functions of the organisation;
- monitoring market trends and competition in the sectors in which the company competes.

## Membership of the Executive Management Committee

- The EMC shall be composed of the chief executive, the chief financial officer (CFO), chief operating officer (COO), and the heads of each of the main functions: HR, risk, ICT, marketing, legal, operations and the Company Secretary.

- From time to time others may be invited by the chief executive to attend all or part of any meeting to present on particular topics or participate in relevant discussions.

## Chair of the Executive Management Committee

- The chief executive shall act as chair of the EMC, or in his or her absence a nominated executive shall act as chair.

## Secretary to the Executive Management Committee

The Company Secretary, or his or her nominee, shall act as the secretary to the EMC.

## Quorum

- The quorum necessary for the transaction of business and taking of key decisions by the EMC shall be [five][5] members, of whom at least one must be either the chief executive or a nominated executive, such as the CFO or the COO. Ideally, the EMC will make all decisions by consensus as 'buy in' by all is very important. However, the EMC should also have the power to decide by a vote, if necessary.

## Frequency of Meetings

The EMC should meet as often as necessary to manage the business effectively. (Every two to four weeks would be the typical frequency.)

## Notice of Meetings

- A schedule of EMC meetings is drawn up at the beginning of the year. Meetings shall be held a number of weeks before board

[5] Square brackets contain recommendations in line with best practice but which may need to be changed to suit the circumstances of the particular organisation, or excluded where not relevant.

meetings to facilitate their preparation. Agendas and supporting papers are sent to each EMC member at least [three] working days before each EMC meeting.
• The chief executive also has the authority to schedule other meetings as and when required.

## Regulation of Meetings

• All EMC meetings shall be conducted in accordance with the provisions of the company's constitution, board policies, best practice in corporate governance and the laws of the land.

## Record of Meetings

• The secretary shall minute the proceedings and decisions of each EMC meeting.
• Minutes of each EMC meeting shall be circulated promptly to all members of the EMC and, once agreed, to all members of the board.
• The attendees of each meeting should also be noted.

## Responsibilities of the EMC

• The exact responsibilities of the EMC will depend on the nature and organisation of the company. The responsibilities below are indicative only and will need to be thought through in detail for each company. These responsibilities are broadly as follows:

### *Strategy*

• Develop and seek approval from the board on corporate objectives and strategy for the company, taking into account the interests of its shareholders, customers, employees and other stakeholder groups. This will include detailed financial and operational budgets for the company.

## *Business Performance*

- Monitoring business and operational performance against objectives, targets and key performance indicators as approved by the board.

## *Functional Responsibilities*

- Each function should draw up its own specific responsibilities and deliverables that are in line with the corporate objectives, the strategic plan and the annual business plan and budget.

## *Policies*

- It will be the job of the EMC to implement company policies approved by the board and to develop policies that are appropriate at EMC level and below.

## *Reporting Responsibilities*

- The chief executive will report in writing to each board meeting on the activities of the EMC since the previous board meeting.

## Other Matters

The EMC shall conduct an annual review of its own performance. This review will cover:

- a review of its charter
- agendas and how time is used
- efficiency of the decision-making process
- the format, quality and clarity of the information presented
- secretarial support and process
- quality of the minutes taken
- etc.

# A5.

# Sample Letter of Non-executive Director Appointment

- Introduction
- Appointment
- Expectations Regarding Time Commitments
- Duties
- Remuneration and Expenses
- Independence and External Interests
- Confidentiality
- Induction
- Annual Performance Reviews
- Training
- Insurance and Indemnity
- Independent Professional Advice
- Personal Details
- Return of Property
- Non-compete
- Data Protection
- Rights of Third Parties
- Law

# Introduction

This sample letter is intended to provide guidance on the points a company may wish to cover in its appointment letters to directors. The text and content should be adapted to suit the company's own circumstances.

I am pleased to confirm that upon the recommendation of the nomination committee, the board has approved your appointment as [an independent/non-independent] non-executive director of [name of company] ("the Company"). This letter sets out the main terms and conditions of your appointment.

It is agreed that, on acceptance of this offer, this letter will constitute a contract for services and not a contract of employment.

# Appointment

Subject to the subsequent provisions of this letter, your appointment is for an initial term of [three] years commencing on [date] [unless terminated earlier by either party giving to the other party [X] month[s'] written notice.

Your appointment is subject to the constitution of the company. Nothing in this letter shall be taken to exclude or vary the terms of the constitution as they apply to you as a director of the company. Your continued appointment as a non-executive director is subject to election by the company's shareholders at the AGM and to re-election at any subsequent AGM at which either the constitution of the company requires, or the board resolves, that you stand for re-election.

If the shareholders do not re-elect you as a director, or you are retired from office under the constitution, your appointment shall terminate automatically, with immediate effect.

Continuation of your contract of appointment is also contingent on satisfactory performance by you as a director and any relevant statutory provisions relating to the removal of a director. You will be subject to annual evaluations which will be directed by the chairman.

Non-executive directors are typically expected to serve [two] ]three-] year terms, but may be invited by the board to serve for an additional period. Any term renewal is subject to board review and the AGM.

You [will/may] be required to serve on one or more committees of the board. You will be provided with the relevant terms of reference on your appointment to such a committee. [You also [will/may] be asked to serve as a senior independent director. Any such appointment will be covered in a separate communication.]

Notwithstanding the paragraphs above, we may terminate your appointment with immediate effect if you:

- commit a material breach of your obligations under this letter;
- commit any serious or repeated breach or non-observance of your obligations to the company;
- are guilty of any fraud or dishonesty or acted in a manner which, in the opinion of the company, brings or is likely to bring you or the company into disrepute or is materially adverse to the interests of the company; or
- are convicted of any criminal offence [other than an offence under the Road Traffic Acts] for which a fine or non-custodial/custodial penalty is imposed; or
- are declared bankrupt or have made an arrangement with or for the benefit of your creditors; or
- are disqualified from acting as a director.

On termination of your appointment, you shall at the request of the company resign from your office as a director of the company.

If there are matters that arise which cause you concern about your role, you should discuss them with me [or the Senior Independent Director].

## Expectations Regarding Time Commitments

You will be expected to devote such time as is necessary for the proper performance of your duties and you should be prepared to spend at least [X] days per [month/year] on company business, including preparation for and attendance at:

- scheduled and unscheduled board meetings;
- board committee meetings, if you are appointed to one;

- board social events, such as dinners;
- annual board strategy 'away-day(s)';
- the AGM/EGM;
- meetings of the non-executive directors;
- meetings with shareholders;
- governance training;
- meetings as part of the board evaluation process.

By accepting this appointment you undertake that, taking into account all other commitments you may have, you are able to, and will, devote sufficient time to your duties as a non-executive director.

## Duties

You will be expected to carry out your duties to a standard commensurate with both the functions of your role, your knowledge, skills and experience.

You will exercise your powers as a non-executive director having regard to relevant obligations under prevailing law and regulation and the appropriate codes of corporate governance.

You will have particular regard to the general duties of directors as set out in the relevant Companies Act/Code of Board Conduct, including the duty to promote the success of the company and, in doing so, have regard (amongst other matters) to:

- the likely consequences of any decision in the short, medium or longer term;
- the interests of the company's employees;
- the need to foster the company's business relationships with suppliers, customers, joint venture partners and others;
- the impact of the company's operations on the community and the environment, as wells as key stakeholders;
- the desirability of the company maintaining a reputation for high standards of business ethics and conduct; and
- the need to act fairly as between members of the company.

In your role as non-executive director you will be required to:

- constructively challenge and help develop proposals on company policy and strategy;

- scrutinise and challenge the performance of the executive management team in meeting agreed goals and objectives, and monitor the reporting of performance;
- satisfy yourself on the integrity of financial information and that financial and other internal controls and systems of risk management are robust and defensible;
- determine the appropriate levels of remuneration of executive directors and have a prime role in appointing and removing executive directors where necessary, and in succession planning;
- devote time to developing and refreshing your knowledge of the environment and the market that the company trades in and your skills;
- uphold high standards of integrity and probity, and support the directors in instilling appropriate ethics, values and behaviours in the company;
- insist on receiving high-quality information sufficiently in advance of board meetings; and
- take into account the views of shareholders and other stakeholders where appropriate.

You will be required to exercise relevant powers under, and abide by, the company's constitution, policies and procedures, and internal control framework.

You will disclose any direct or indirect interest you may have in any matter being considered at a board meeting or a committee meeting.

Unless specifically authorised to do so by the board, you will not enter into any legal or other commitment or contract on behalf of the company.

## Remuneration and Expenses

The annual fee rate as at the date of this letter is [€XX,XXX] gross per annum, paid [monthly] in arrears. This fee covers all duties, including service on any board committee, with the exception of committee chairmanships and certain additional responsibilities, such as the role of Senior Independent Director. [All fees will be paid through PAYE and are subject to income tax and other statutory deductions.]

Directors' fees will be subject to an annual review by the remuneration committee.

The company will reimburse you for all reasonable and properly documented expenses incurred in carrying out your duties. The procedure and other guidance in respect of expense claims is set out in [name of document]. Expenses will be paid monthly in arrears.

On termination of this appointment, you shall only be entitled to such fees as may have accrued to the date of termination, together with reimbursement in the normal way of any expenses properly incurred prior to that date.

## Independence and External Interests

You have already disclosed to the board the significant commitments you have outside this role. You must inform me in advance of any changes to these commitments that might impact on the time that you are able to devote to your role as director of the company.

In the event that you become aware of any potential or actual conflicts of interest, these should be disclosed to me and the Company Secretary as soon as they become apparent. It may be necessary to get the agreement of the board.

## Confidentiality

You acknowledge that all information acquired during your appointment is confidential to the company and should not be released, communicated, disclosed, during your appointment or following termination (by whatever means), to third parties without approval from the company.

You acknowledge the need to hold and retain company information under appropriately secure conditions.

## Induction

The company will provide a comprehensive, formal induction programme. You will be expected to make yourself available during your first year of appointment for not less than an additional [XX] days for the purposes of the induction.

## Annual Performance Reviews

The performance of individual directors, and the whole board and its committees, is evaluated annually under the direction of the chairman.

## Training

The company will facilitate training opportunities for you to develop and refresh your skills and knowledge relevant to you carrying out your duties effectively. You should endeavour to make yourself available for any relevant training session.

## Insurance and Indemnity

The company has taken out director and officer liability insurance and it is intended to maintain such cover for the full term of your appointment. You have been informed of the current indemnity limit, on which the board is updated from time to time. A copy of the policy will be provided to you on request.

You will also be granted a deed of indemnity by the company.

## Independent Professional Advice

A copy of the board's agreed procedure under which directors may obtain independent advice will be provided by the Company Secretary. The company will reimburse reasonable costs incurred by you in accordance with its policy.

## Personal Details

You shall advise the Company Secretary promptly of any change in address or other personal contact details.

## Return of Property

Upon termination of your appointment with the company, you shall return all documents, records, papers or other company property that may be in your possession or under your control, and which relate in any way to the business affairs of the company.

## Non-compete

By countersignature of this letter you now agree that you will not (without the previous consent in writing of the company), for the period of [XX] months immediately after the termination of your office, carry on or be engaged, concerned or interested in any business that is similar to or competes with any business being carried on by the company.

## Data Protection

By signing this letter, you consent to the company holding and processing information about you for legal, personnel, administrative and management purposes and in particular to the processing of any sensitive personal data, as and when appropriate.

## Rights of Third Parties

No person other than you and the company shall have any rights under this letter and the terms of this letter shall not be enforceable by any person other than you and the company.

## Law

Your engagement with the company is governed by and shall be construed in accordance with the laws of [country] and your engagement shall be subject to the jurisdiction of the courts of [country].

This letter constitutes the entire terms and conditions of your appointment and no waiver or modification thereof shall be valid unless in writing and signed by the parties hereto.

If you are willing to accept these terms of appointment, please confirm your acceptance by signing and returning to me the enclosed copy of this letter.

Yours sincerely [name] Chairman

---

I confirm and agree to the terms of my appointment as a non-executive director of [name of company] as set out in this letter.

---

[name]

---

[date]

# A6.

# Sample Outline for an Organisation's Code of Ethics

- Introduction
- Stakeholder Groups that should be Covered by a Code of Ethics
- Description of the Ethics and Compliance Programme
- Supporting/Related Policies and Procedures
- Supporting Resources

## Introduction

The purpose of this appendix is to provide a suggested outline to an organisation's code of ethics. The final structure, content and tone of the code will be influenced by the history of the company and its board. The executives nominated to develop a draft of the code would need to do the appropriate research using this index as a guide.

- Letter from Chairman or Chief Executive
- Objectives of Code of Business Conduct
- Statement of core beliefs or values.

## Stakeholder Groups that should be Covered by a Code of Ethics

- Customers
- Shareholders/investors
- Suppliers/service providers
- Staff
- The company
- The community.

## Description of the Ethics and Compliance Programme

- Responsible senior executive and staff
- Communications plan
- Monitoring and auditing processes
- How to seek advice and report breaches of the code
- Investigations process
- Dispute-resolution process
- Tracking, measuring and reporting
- Programme evaluation and modification process
- Annual Ethics Report (the purpose of the Annual Ethics Report is to report to the various stakeholder groups on how the company has performed against its code of ethics).

## Supporting/Related Policies and Procedures

- Business Ethics Officer: duties and responsibilities
- Monitoring and auditing policy
- Investigations policy
- Confidentiality policy
- Whistle-blower policies (problem reporting and non-retaliation policies)
- Helpline policy and procedures
- Confidentiality agreements, including whistle-blowing
- Education and training policies
- Response, follow-up and resolution policies.

## Supporting Resources

- Guides to ethical decision making
- Key contact details
- Case studies
- Ethics games (which could include role-playing scenarios)
- Samples of other codes of ethics from benchmark organisations
- Online resource centre.

# A7.
## Case Studies

- **The Abbey Theatre**
- **FÁS**
- **Irish Nationwide Building Society**
- **Neath vs Ospreys**
- **Tallaght Hospital**

# THE ABBEY THEATRE

## Key Issue

- Deficiencies in internal financial controls and financial reporting systems.

## Context

The Abbey Theatre is the national theatre of Ireland. In 1925 it became the first ever state-subsidised theatre in the English-speaking world.

The National Theatre Society Limited was incorporated and founded in 1904 and had various mechanisms of appointing and selecting board members. The Advisory Council elected four members to the board and was comprised of representatives of the artistic, theatre, business and trade union community. Two others were nominated by the Minister for Arts, Sport and Tourism, while one was a staff council representative, one an Actors' Equity representative and one a playwright. That is how the composition of the board was made up.

Representation on the board was disparate. The Chairman of the board of the National Theatre Society Limited was elected by the board members, rather than being appointed. There was a finance and audit control committee of the board, but there were concerns at board level that information was not being made available quickly enough.

Following the discovery of under-recording of an emerging deficit in the organisation's accounts for 2004,[1] the Managing and Artistic Directors stepped down.

At the heart of the crisis was the fact that the theatre lost €1.85 million in 2004, its centenary year, which was more than double the expected figure.[2] An overly ambitious centenary programme, a hugely expensive production of *The Shaughraun* by Dion Boucicault

---

[1] Committee of Public Accounts, 24 November 2005.
[2] See Maeve Sheehan, "The €1.85m splurge that has laid the Abbey Theatre bare", *Irish Independent*, 15 May 2005.

and a serious miscalculation of the cost of touring J.M. Synge's *The Playboy of the Western World* were blamed for the black hole in the accounts, which left the Abbey struggling with a total operating deficit of €3.4 million at the end of the year in question.

> "Official explanations sounded glib. A combination of 'system failure' and 'human error' had caused the money to slip through the net, a spokesman for the Abbey later said …".[3]

The Director of the Arts Council described the disclosure of the new losses as "a bolt from the blue" at the time and a cause of deep concern. (The Arts Council is responsible for funding, developing and promoting the Arts in Ireland.)

## Governance Issues

- The board commissioned independent consultants (KPMG) to review the Abbey's accounting and financial control systems and to ascertain how the scale of the shortfall was underestimated by management and the board.[4]
- The KPMG report on the crisis was critical of the Abbey board for not exercising more effective oversight of the theatre's financial reporting and cost controls, particularly in relation to the centenary programme. It detailed poor corporate governance, accounting errors, faulty accounting systems, inadequately trained staff and ad hoc financial analysis as contributing to the scale of the problem. It recommended a series of sweeping changes, including significant redundancies where headcount would fall by 30 staff out of a total of 91 over 16 months.[5] It also found that where actual costs or revenue figures were not available, estimates were used to support forecasts which turned out to be unreliable.
- The KPMG report made it clear that there was no evidence of theft or fraud and no suggestion of misconduct by any member of the board or finance committee. However, the report also stated that it found five separate Abbey budgets for the year under review,

---

[3] Maeve Sheehan, *Irish Independent*, 15 May 2005.
[4] Committee of Public Accounts 24 November 2005.
[5] See Maeve Sheehan, *Irish Independent*, 15 May 2005.

all with different projected outcomes, and added that the income and expenditure statements for the first four months of the year were "incomplete and unreliable". The KPMG report also pointed the finger at, *inter alia*, the board, the finance audit committee and management.

- The failure of the board of the Abbey to correctly gauge the level of the organisation's deficit was blamed on its financial reporting system.
- The Minister, who received a copy of the external consultants' report, said it appeared there had been "gross incompetence" in the management of the theatre's finances.
- On 20 August 2005, the Abbey Theatre Advisory Council approved a plan to dissolve the Abbey's owner, the National Theatre Society Limited, and replace it with a company limited by guarantee, the Abbey Theatre Limited, and a new board.

## Key Lessons

There are many lessons to be learnt from the Abbey Theatre case, but the key ones are:

- The board of the National Theatre Society Limited may not have had the appropriate skills and expertise to ensure that there was the appropriate financial oversight of the Abbey Theatre's finances, given the way members were appointed or elected to it and their differing backgrounds.
- A board must ensure that there is an appropriate system of financial control in place which is appropriate to the organisation.
- The Abbey's budgeting and management accounting systems lacked rigour and formality. However, it is unclear if budgets were signed off formally by the board or not, or indeed if they were part of the financial reporting system. Given this, the key lesson for any board is to ensure that there is a fit-for-purpose management reporting and budgetary system.
- The necessity for accurate and timely management information is critical in running any enterprise. In particular, it is imperative that the accounting policies and budgetary assumptions underpinning them are agreed and understood.

# FÁS

## Key Issue

- Deficiencies in internal financial controls and financial reporting systems

## Context

FÁS (Foras Áiseanna Saothair) was a statutory body tasked with training persons who are unemployed, as well as the upskilling of people in employment and administrative apprenticeships.

In 2006, it had a board consisting of a chairman, 16 ordinary members, including five ministerial appointments, and two FÁS employees. It had seven subcommittees and three advisory committees dealing with apprenticeships, the construction and engineering industries.

The board met 10 times per annum in addition to one meeting devoted to strategy.

It also had an executive board comprised of a Director General and seven assistant director generals. It had no formal terms of reference.

## Governance Issues

- The Irish Comptroller & Auditor General (C&AG) examined the processing of transactions at FÁS head office and the governance arrangements of the organisation. This was a follow-up to a Special Report[6] carried out in 2009.
- The C&AG report[7] found that FÁS had a governance structure that was consistent with its governing legislation and with the

---

[6] Comptroller and Auditor General, *Advertising and Promotion in FÁS* (Special Report Number 66, 2009).
[7] Comptroller and Auditor General, *Internal Control and Governance in FÁS* (December 2009).

*Code of Practice for the Governance of State Bodies.*[8] It also had a plan of control, which, if fully implemented, would have provided sufficient assurance that its transactions were processed in a safe and timely manner.

- However, failure to fully implement elements of the plan of control exposed FÁS to the risk of losses as well as failing to achieve the best value for money. The exposures arose from the fact that:
  - authorisation limits were breached when certain transactions were initiated;
  - there were deficiencies in the conduct of tender processes when goods and services were being acquired;
  - payments were made in the absence of supporting documentation;
  - confirmation orders for purchases already effected were issued in many instances;
  - the system of risk management adopted by the board did not function effectively.
- A number of specific findings included:
  - Risk management:
    - the board approved a risk management policy in 2005, but it was not operated as intended. Risk registers and action plans were not kept up to date, reporting procedures as envisaged by the policy were not operated and there were no annual reviews of the effectiveness of the risk management system.
  - Internal financial control:
    - FÁS had a system of control that was adequate but did not always operate effectively and as intended.
- Communication between control units:
  - One of the reasons the internal control framework did not operate effectively was the poor level of communication between the procurement and the financial accounting functions.
  - Internal audit:
    - The audit committee had the responsibility with management to review the activities of the internal audit function. An external review of the internal audit function found *inter alia*, that not all of its recommendations were implemented in a timely manner.

---

[8] *Code of Practice for the Governance of State Bodies*, Department of Finance, October 2001 and updated in June 2009.

○ Board information:
  ♦ Financial information presented to the FÁS board was sufficient to allow it to identify variances from budget at programme level, but not at activity below that level. The board was not aware of overspends on advertising and promotion, although the executive was.

## Key Lessons

The lesson for boards from the C&AG's report on FÁS are many and varied. Some of the key ones are as follows:

- Before agreeing to join the board of any organisation, a potential member should carry out due diligence to provide the comfort that it has the appropriate internal control framework and that the reporting systems are in place to provide the evidence that they function effectively.
- Board members must be actively involved in ensuring that the appropriate internal controls and procedures are in place either by asking the right questions at board level or by being involved on a committee with the appropriate terms of reference and/or seeking backing evidence of assurances made.
- The audit committee should ensure that there are processes in place to ensure that the right level of detail of financial information is provided at committee level and board level so that key variances are understood.
- If a board member does not have the appropriate degree of confidence in the internal control systems, he or she should request a review by an independent third party with the appropriate skills and experience to do so.
- Board members should insist that risk assurance is kept as a live item on the board's agenda and monitored appropriately.
- Government should ensure there is a rigorous selection process in place to ensure that the right skills and experience are around the boardroom table to ask the hard questions.
- An annual review of the information provided to a board and how it is presented should be conducted to ensure that it (or its committees) has the right information to ensure that it can do its job. This task is too often left to the executive.

# IRISH NATIONWIDE BUILDING SOCIETY

## Key Issue

- Inappropriate and inadequate corporate governance structures for an organisation of its type.

## Context

The Irish Nationwide Building Society (INBS) was originally regulated by the Registrar of Friendly Societies, but the duty fell on the Central Bank of Ireland in 1989 and then the Financial Regulator in 2004.

In 2004, the INBS had a board of four members comprising a chairman, one non-executive director and two executive directors, one of whom was the chief executive and the other was the CFO and Company Secretary. It also had an internal audit committee and a credit committee.

There was a management team of 12 people who reported to the chief executive.

The INBS had a loan book of nearly €12 billion and profits peaked at €391 million in 2007.

In August 2010, INBS required a €5.4 billion bailout from the Irish Government to stay afloat, leaving it effectively in State ownership. Many of these loans were sanctioned by the chief executive. Relative to its size, INBS is proportionately the biggest banking collapse in the history of Irish State.

## Governance Issues

- An investigation by KPMG[9] found that the chief executive had been granted special powers by the board of the society as far back as 1981. These powers were reinforced by the board in December 1994 and again in August 1997.[10]

---

[9] Tom Lyons, *The Irish Times,* 3 July 2014.
[10] Tom Lyons and Richard Curran, *Fingers: The Man Who Brought Down Irish Nationwide and Cost us €5.4Bn* (Gill and Macmillan, 2011).

- These measures empowered the chief executive to[11]:
  - set, vary or alter interest rates and fees;
  - make arrangements with individual members of the society;
  - charge different people different rates of interest;
  - structure a commercial or residential loan with one customer on certain conditions, such as interest-only for a decade, and on completely different terms with others;
  - change the rates or the conditions attached to the loan at will. Thus, having lent out €1 million at a certain rate and repayable at a certain time in the future, he could then alter those conditions at any stage as he saw fit. He did not need to consult the board or anyone else to do this.
- By granting these powers the board was giving the chief executive the autonomy and authority to do deals with virtually anyone he wished, amend any deal he wanted and run the INBS as a personal fiefdom without, it would appear, breaking any of its rules. The normal checks and balances of having a chairman, a board with the appropriate skills and experience, an audit committee, a credit committee, were de facto irrelevant. It was a total abrogation of its statutory and fiduciary duties by the board, which has been described as "dysfunctional".[12] Consequently, the chief executive, given his "special powers", had no accountability for his actions to the board of INBS.
- One of the non-executive directors who sat on the board for six years was not aware of these powers, which seems unusual.
- The Irish Nationwide structure revealed a number of things:
  - Despite being regulated by the Central Bank and subsequently by the Financial Regulator in 2004:
    - the autonomy delegated by the board to the chief executive does not seem to have been raised as an issue,
    - it would appear that the make-up and size of the board was never questioned.
  - The chief executive was all-powerful.
- One of the effects of this structure was that there was no proper senior management team familiar with different parts of the business. In fact, one experienced senior manager from another

---

[11] *Ibid.*
[12] "10 things We Learned from RTE's Inside Irish Nationwide", *The Journal*, 12 February 2013.

financial institution had joined INBS, but left over governance concerns. The chief executive was the only person who knew everything. The organisation was run in silos and as there was no senior management team, there was no real sharing of information, which would have been normal in other institutions.

- It is difficult to believe that a board would allow a chief executive to oversee a loan book of nearly €12 billion and make decisions about changes to the terms and conditions for major borrowers without board oversight.

## Key Lessons

While the governance issues and lessons arising as a result of the INBS debacle could fill a book, some of the more relevant are as follows:

- The board of INBS was too small to perform its role. A board of four members (at times six), two of whom were executive directors, was too small to ensure appropriate governance at INBS. Typically, non-executive directors play a major role in board committees, such as audit, risk, nomination, credit (in the case of financial institutions), etc. With only two non-executive directors at INBS, resourcing these committees adequately would have been impossible.
- A financial institution also needs to have the appropriate skills and experience round the boardroom table to enable it to perform its role. Many of these were clearly absent at INBS. Such skills and experience could range from legal, banking, governance, regulatory, economic, key sectors of the economy, etc.
- Board policies must be transparent to all board members, should be reviewed on a regular basis and be readily available.
- There needs to be absolute clarity on the decision-making authority of the board, board committees, the chief executive, the executive management team and internal committees.
- There should be a defined management structure with clear roles, responsibilities and reporting arrangements.
- There should be regular rotation of board members.
- The chief executive should have his or her performance reviewed annually.

# NEATH VS OSPREYS

## Key Issue

• Multiple directors and overlapping interests.

## Context

Investors will often find themselves in a position where they are not only an investor but also a director (including non-executive, executive and shadow directors) of a company. As a result, it is possible for competing interests to arise between the interests of the investor and the affairs of the company.

As well as being mindful of any remedies a company may have against a director for breach of duty, an investor who is also a director must also be careful to ensure that his or her conduct does not fall foul of section 994 of the Companies Act 2006 (UK), i.e. that the company's affairs are being or have been conducted in a manner which is unfairly prejudicial to the interests of some or all of its members. (The equivalent provision in Irish law is section 205 of the Companies Act 1963.)

Care must be taken when an investor has multiple directorships, including non-executive roles, because at some point the proper performance of his or her duties for one company may adversely affect the interests of another.

The Court of Appeal in the UK considered this question in the case of *Hawkes v. Cuddy*.[13]

In this case, Mr Cuddy's wife and Mr Hawkes were directors in Neath Rugby Ltd ("Neath"), which owned Neath Rugby Club. Although Mrs Cuddy was named as a director (alongside Mr Hawkes), it was in fact her husband, Mr Cuddy, who acted as if he were a director; he was therefore a de facto director (a person acting as a director, who is not validly appointed) of Neath.

Neath decided that it would form a new rugby club, the Ospreys by forming a joint venture company with Swansea Rugby Club. Mr Cuddy and Mr Hawkes agreed that Mr Hawkes would

---

[13] [2009] EWCA Civ 291 (see www.casetrack.com/ct4plc.nsf/items/1-520-5114)

concentrate on the management of Neath Rugby Club, with Mr Cuddy managing Ospreys and Neath's interests in Ospreys. After some time, Mr Hawkes and Mr Cuddy had a disagreement about the operation of Neath and Ospreys. Mr Hawkes accused Mr Cuddy of failing to promote Neath's interests and Mr Hawkes lodged an unfair prejudice (section 994) petition against Mr Cuddy.

On the facts of the case, it was decided that, in relation to some aspects of his conduct, Mr Cuddy had acted in an unfairly prejudicial manner; for example, Mr Cuddy had used confidential accounting information (obtained by his wife) to assist Ospreys in a trademark infringement claim against Neath. Clearly, this was a breach of Mr Cuddy's duties as a director of Neath as the information used was potentially harmful to Neath.

As well as reaching a decision based on the facts of the case, the Court also gave more general guidance in relation to the position of a director with multiple roles. In relation to a joint venture company, where an individual may be nominated by a shareholder company as a director of the joint venture company, the Court emphasised that a director owes duties to the joint venture company of which he is a director.

In that capacity, he does not owe duties to the shareholder company which nominated him as a director by virtue of that nomination alone. In other words, his duty is to the company to which he has been nominated and not to the company that nominated him.

In terms of multiple directorships, the Court stated that if a director of Company A, when making a decision or acting in a particular way, is not in breach of his duties owed to Company B, then such a decision or action should not be deemed unfairly prejudicial, regardless of the impact on Company B, i.e. the director must put Company A first and Company B second in terms of his duties and responsibilities.

## Governance Issues

In light of this guidance, directors should consider the following:

- the importance of having clear written statements of responsibility;
- amending the company's constitution to allow directors to have additional directorships (actual or potential conflicts, if brought to the attention of the board, can be specifically consented to);

- reviewing the company's director and officer liability insurance;
- ensuring that decisions taken that may affect other companies with which a director is involved (in whatever capacity) are properly discussed, agreed and minuted at board meetings.

## Key Lessons

Lessons for boards from the *Hawkes v. Cuddy* case are as follows:

- In considering the development of a new board or the appointment of new directors to a board, the promoters or the nomination committee should take into account any potential conflicts of interest that could arise.
- At the beginning of each board meeting the chair should ask, based on the proposed agenda, if there are any potential conflicts amongst the directors present so that any conflict can be managed appropriately.
- If there is any doubt about the role of a director on a board where there are multiple and potentially conflicting directorships around the boardroom table, the directors involved should make it clear at all stages in the board meeting which 'hat' they are wearing and ensure that this in minuted when necessary.
- Critically, this should include noting that in discussing any conflict arising, the relevant conflicted directors should absent themselves from any discussion by leaving the meeting.

# TALLAGHT HOSPITAL

## Key Issue

- Inadequate governance for an organisation of its size and complexity.

## Context

- The Adelaide and Meath Hospital, Dublin, incorporating the National Children's Hospital (AMNCH) in Tallaght, Dublin, was established as an entity on 1 August 1996 to provide services on behalf of the Health Services Executive (HSE).
- The hospital is an acute general hospital for both adults and children, with 615 beds. It provides elective and emergency adult and paediatric services on an inpatient, day case and outpatient basis.
- The hospital was previously run by a 23-member board whose general function was to manage its activities and the services provided by it, functions which would not be in line with the principles of modern corporate governance.[14]
- In the period from approximately 2009 to 2011, a number of major issues arose at Tallaght Hospital which resulted in reports being commissioned by the board over concerns about the existing governance arrangements. These reviews were carried out by external consultants.

## *The Hayes Review*

The Hayes Review of 2010[15] looked into the issue of unreported X-rays and unprocessed GP referral letters and recommended operational and governance changes in the wake of this particular scandal.

---

[14] *Report of the investigation into the quality, safety, and governance of the care provided by the Adelaide and Meath Hospital, Dublin, incorporating the National Children's Hospital (AMNCH) for patients who require acute admission* (HIQA, 2012) ('The HIQA Report'), p. 49.

[15] *Report of the Review of Radiology Reporting and the Management of GP Referral Letters at Adelaide and Meath Hospital (Dublin), incorporating the National Children's Hospital (AMNCH) [Tallaght Hospital]* (HSE, 2010) ('The Hayes Report').

This review was prompted by reports in the media that there were (a) 57,000 unreported X-rays and (b) some 30,000 "unopened" or "unprocessed" GP referral letters in Tallaght Hospital. The review queried why the hospital's managers and governors did so little to avert the X-ray and referral letter crisis.

## The Health Information and Quality Agency (HIQA) Review[16]

- A 65-year-old male patient had to endure being treated in a corridor adjacent to an overcrowded Accident & Emergency Department at Tallaght Hospital. Having attended the hospital with severe ankle pain, and having been forced to sit on a chair throughout his stay, he eventually died in undignified, unsanitary and unsafe conditions.
- Two "unexpected deaths", including the case referred to above, occurred at the hospital in March and July respectively in 2011.
- The "unexpected deaths" of the patients in March 2011 led to a Health Information and Quality Agency (HIQA) review into how Tallaght treated patients in its A&E department (the 'HIQA Report').

## Governance Issues

The findings of the HIQA Report on Tallaght Hospital revealed the following key issues:

## The Board

- The board of the hospital did not have effective arrangements in place to adequately direct and govern the hospital, nor did it function in an effective way.
- The Charter or constitution of the hospital was not in line with modern corporate governance principles.
- The amalgamated organisation, into which three separate hospitals – the Adelaide, Meath and National Children's Hospitals – were merged in 1996, continued to embrace a number of different legacy beliefs, activities and cultures, lacked an organisation-wide strategic vision and culture and failed to adequately respond to

---

[16] The HIQA Report, see above.

the significant changes in healthcare delivery as well as advances in modern corporate governance.

- The collective membership of the board did not reflect the relevant diversity of knowledge, skills and competencies required to carry out the full range of oversight responsibilities necessary for a hospital in today's corporate governance environment. Nor was the appointment process in line with modern governance principles.
- The Charter provided for the establishment of a number of committees, which were required to report to the board in relation to their activities. These committees included clinical governance, resource and audit. In 2009 the board commissioned an external review of the governance arrangements at the hospital. As a result of this review, a transitional board of management, which was a sub-committee of the main board of the hospital, was established in 2010 to manage the activities of the hospital.
- These board committees, with the exception of the transitional board of management, had no executive powers but rather advised, reported to and made recommendations to the board. In addition, information came to the attention of the HIQA during its review that raised concerns about the effectiveness of the governance arrangements in place for financial management, financial transparency and commitment control. In particular, HIQA was concerned that the hospital did not have the internal controls in place to ensure its compliance with public procurement legislation.
- In October 2011, HIQA had significant concerns in relation to the corporate and clinical governance arrangements in place at the hospital and, in particular, the effectiveness of the board's governance arrangements. The Authority met with the Minister for Health to advise him of these concerns and subsequently issued preliminary draft recommendations to the Minister to help mitigate the risks at that time. The hospital also had substantial financial difficulties with a significant budgetary overrun.
- In addition, there was also a lack of accountability within the hospital regarding €740,000 in additional payments to senior staff (one staff member got an extra €150,000 in 'top-up' pay). HIQA said it was not clear how decisions were made, and on what basis, to pay out these monies.

- There were also procurement issues in relation to €1.8 million of consultancy services, which were not put out to tender, nor did the board approve the amount of the expenditure.[17]
- On 9 November 2011, the Minister for Health and the Church of Ireland Archbishop of Dublin announced a series of new initiatives to reform and modernise the governance structures of the hospital over two phases. The Archbishop was involved given that the Adelaide Hospital had a Church of Ireland origin and ethos and was one of the three hospitals that merged to form AMNCH. The first phase involved a further reduction in the size of the hospital board occurring through the appointment of an interim board of 16 members and, in the longer term, the Charter was to be replaced. The first meeting of the new interim board took place on 21 December 2011, with new members being nominated on the basis of their competencies to undertake the role.
- HIQA's report of 8 May 2012 subsequently recommended that the board should be of a sufficient size (up to a maximum of 12 members) to effectively govern the organisation, and that all members should be non-executive members.

### Executive Management

- The executive management arrangements at the hospital had, over three years prior to the publication of the HIQA Report, gone through a number of significant changes, with four members of staff acting in the role of chief executive at different times in that three-year period. There was no clear scheme of delegation from the board to the chief executive or to the executive management team for accountability in relation to the delivery and performance of the hospital's functions.
- There was ambiguity as to who had overall executive accountability for the quality and safety of the services delivered, and an apparent lack of integration across those corporate and clinical governance arrangements that were in place. The effective management arrangements that were needed to facilitate the delivery of high quality, safe and reliable care and support, by allocating the necessary resources through informed decisions and actions, were not sufficiently in place.

---

[17] See www.irishhealth.com, 2 November 2012.

- HIQA found that, historically, there was evidence that the hospital had not adequately planned or controlled the scope or expansion of the clinical services provided. However, there was evidence that the hospital was developing programmes for improvement, including policies and programmes to deliver improvement in Out-Patients Department (OPD) turnaround times, bed management and patient discharge planning.
- The turnover of senior executives at the hospital, and the ongoing 'acting' status of individuals in key positions, created challenges in leadership, management, stability, decision-making, confidence and authority. This had the potential to impact on the ability of the hospital to effectively address the quality, safety and financial challenges that it faced.

## Key Lessons

- The governance issues identified at Tallaght Hospital were fundamental and eventually catastrophic. As identified by the HIQA Report, though there were many early warning signs that all was not well, these were either ignored by the board or the board did not have the competencies to recognise that there were serious governance issues. The link between good governance and patient safety did not appear to have been made by the board members. It was only when major issues surfaced that action was taken by the competent authorities. It is probably safe to assume that the malaise did not develop overnight and was a result of governance structures which were clearly not fit for purpose.
- The governance issues stem from a board that did not appear to have the skills and experience to ensure that the appropriate governance and management structures, processes and procedures were put in place at the hospital. Good corporate governance begins and ends with the board. This did not seem to be the case at Tallaght despite, no doubt, the good intentions of all the board members concerned.

# Useful Websites

www.charteredaccountants.ie Visit the Chartered Accountants Ireland website to view the corporate governance resource.

www.cgai.ie The Corporate Governance Association of Ireland is the professional association of members certified in corporate governance postgraduate studies.

www.corporategovernance.ie The IoD/UCD Centre for Corporate Governance.

www.cimaglobal.com A selection of topics covered, e.g. regarding non-executive directors.

www.cro.ie The Companies Office – a number of useful papers available for downloading.

www.frc.org.uk/publications Including the *UK Corporate Governance Code*.

www.icsa.org.uk Offers guidelines for NEDs and other key elements in the corporate governance framework.

www.independentdirector.co.uk Offers guidelines on corporate governance.

www.iodireland.ie The Institute of Directors in Ireland (IOD).

www.odce.ie Office of the Director of Corporate Enforcement. Full list of legislation governing companies in the Republic of Ireland, including all relevant statutory instruments.

# Index